German Castles

Gast im Schloss

Ein Reise(ver)führer zu Burgen, Schlössern, Herrenhäusern und Klöstern in Deutschland

ReiseArt®

Nicole Schmidt, Michael Maaß

Gast im Schloss
Ein Reise(ver)führer zu
Burgen, Schlössern, Herrenhäusern
und Klöstern in Deutschland

ISBN 3-937939-02-4

The prices listed are recommended prices.

*) Service number of the DTAG 0,12 €/min
from the German fixed network

Schillerstaße 17, 99423 Weimar
Tel.: +49 (0) 36 43-81 17 10, Fax: +49 (0) 36 43-81 17 19
E-Mail: info@reiseart.com, http://www.reiseart.com

In Zusammenarbeit mit "Gast im Schloss e.V."
c/o Jagdschloss Kranichstein, Darmstadt

Layout: MEDIENSERVICE MATHIAS KARGE, Erfurt; mathias@karge.com

Translation: Worldwide Business Centres Erfurt, erfurt@wwbc.de

Herstellung: Media Kontor Stuttgart GmbH

Printed in Austria; Friedrich VDV, Linz

German Castles

Gast im Schloss

Ein Reise(ver)führer zu Burgen, Schlössern,
Herrenhäusern und Klöstern in Deutschland

ReiseArt®

Heimbs
KAFFEE

German Castles

GAST IM SCHLOSS

DIE „GAST IM SCHLOSS“ PHILOSOPHIE

THE “GAST IM SCHLOSS” PHILOSOPHY

Gast im Schloss – nicht nur eine zeitlose aktuelle Hotelidee, sondern die Kreation eines besonderen Lebensgefühls voller Komfort und Atmosphäre hinter geschichtsträchtigen Mauern, jung im Geist, stilbewusst in der historischen Ausstattung und einzigartig in der individuellen Handschrift des jeweiligen Objekts und seiner Betreiber. Herzlich willkommen bei – Gast im Schloss – der traditionsreichen Kooperation für Hotels und Restaurants in deutschen Burgen, Schlössern, Klöstern und Herrenhäusern.

Seit mehr als 40 Jahren spannt Gast im Schloss den Bogen zwischen den Gästen und den signifikanten Zeugen eines reichen Erbes, den Schlössern, Burgen, Klöstern und Herrenhäusern in unserem Lande. Besonders in der heutigen Zeit, in der nur noch der Maßstab „schneller, höher, weiter“ zu gelten scheint, ist es wichtig, sich auch einmal eine Ruhepause zu gönnen. Das Erlebnis als Gast im Schloss möge Sie verzaubern und auffangen in einer Welt voller Faszination. Die Tore sind für Sie weit geöffnet. Herzlich willkommen.

“Gast im Schloss” is not only a timeless idea of today, but the creation of a special feeling for life, integrated with modern comfort and atmosphere behind historical foundations. The concept is built upon young ideals combined with an awareness for style in a setting of hisorical surroundings in the unique signature of these properties and their owners/managers. We welcome you to the “Gast im Schloss” – the traditional cooperation for hotels and restaurants in German castles, palaces, monasteries, mansions and country estates.

For more than 40 years “Gast im Schloss” brings, our pretentious guests, the rich inheritance of the palaces, castles, monasteries, mansions and estates in Germany. Especially today, where things are measured by their importance for being “faster, higher and better”, it is most important that we allow ourselves a quiet break from the daily stress and routine. The enchanting experience that our hotels do offer, will captivate you into a world of facination. The doors are wide open to welcome you.

EINLEITUNG

INTRODUCTION

Jahr für Jahr kommen tausende von Besuchern nach Deutschland, weil sie die hier vorhandene Vielfalt historischer Gebäude lieben und deren Charme erleben möchten. Schlösser und Burgen, Herrenhäuser und Klöster stehen, neben weitgehend erhaltenen historischen Stadtkernen und romantischen Landschaften, ganz oben in der Gunst der Besucher. Einige dieser einst dem Adel vorbehaltenen Gebäude, sind heute Hotels, die ihren Gästen auch längere Aufenthalte in angenehmer Umgebung ermöglichen. Beim einheimischen Publikum erfreut sich das Übernachten in ehemals herrschaftlichen Gebäuden ebenfalls zunehmender Beliebtheit. In den letzten Jahren wurde eine

Fond of the existing variety of historical buildings here and keen to experience their charm, thousands of visitors come year after year to Germany. Castles, manor houses and monasteries, also well preserved historical town centres and romantic landscapes are on the top of visitors' lists of 'must-sees'. Some of these once aristocratic buildings, are today hotels, which provide pleasant surroundings for guests on both shorter and longer breaks. It is likewise becoming more popular for locals to stay overnight in these former stately buildings. In recent years a large number of former manors and castles have been transformed into

Vielzahl früherer Landgüter, Schlösser und Burgen einer neuen Nutzung als Hotel zugeführt. So gibt es heute in Deutschland flächendeckend, mit kleinen regionalen Schwerpunkten, ein breites Angebot herrschaftlicher Anwesen, in denen man übernachten und sich wohl fühlen kann. Der vorliegende Reise(ver)-

hotels. There is therefore a wide range of stately homes situated throughout Germany, with small regional emphasis, where you can stay overnight and feel at home. This guidebook presents a small, but quite delightful selection of these hotels. They all cooperate with one another in order to ensure that the

führer präsentiert eine kleine, aber durchaus reizvolle Auswahl dieser Häuser. Sie alle kooperieren miteinander, um dem „Gast im Schloss" einen möglichst angenehmen und einprägsamen Aufenthalt zu ermöglichen. Durch ihre meist familiäre, individuelle Führung heben sie sich, kategorieunabhängig, deutlich von der üblichen Hotellerie ab.

Da alle Hotels in überaus kulturträchtigen Regionen und Orten liegen, ist auch bei

castle guest has the most pleasant and memorable stay possible. Regardless of their star rating, most of the hotels provide family-run, individual management, that clearly stands out from the usual run-of-the-mill businesses in the hotel trade.

Since all the hotels are situated in extremely culturally rich regions and locations, plenty of variety is on offer to satisfy even those on longer breaks.

längeren Aufenthalten für ausreichend Abwechslung gesorgt. Unsere Tipps und Themen-Spezials verweisen auf die jeweiligen Angebote und Möglichkeiten. Umgeben von geschichtsträchtigen Mauern, geschmackvollem Interieur, historischen Parks und Schlossgärten bieten alle Hotels auch individuelle Hochzeits- und Fest-Arrangements an. Diese sind so unterschiedlich wie die Häuser selbst und immer ein einzigartiges Erlebnis. Zahl-

Our tips and topical specials correspond with the respective special offers and possibilities. Surrounded by historical walls, tasteful interiors, historical parks and castle gardens, all the hotels also offer individual wedding and party arrangements. These vary as much as the hotels themselves and always provide an unique experience. Numerous ball and event rooms are inviting locations for any type of cele-

reiche Fest- und Veranstaltungsräume laden hierbei zum Feiern ein. Viele Hotels verfügen zudem über ein Standesamt, eine Kapelle oder Kirche und natürlich über romantische Hochzeitssuiten. Kutschenfahrten werden ebenso angeboten wie ein krönendes Feuerwerk auf dem Höhepunkt des Festes.

Wo einst Ritter, Mönche und Edelleute an schweren Eichentischen beisammen saßen, bieten die historischen Schlösser, Burgen, Klöster und Herrenhäuser den idealen Rahmen für anspruchsvolle

bration. Many hotels have a registry office, a chapel or church at their disposal and of course romantic marriage suites. Traditional coach rides are on offer, as are the crowning fireworks at the height of the celebrations.

Where once knights, monks and noblemen sat together at heavy oak tables, the historical castle, monastery and manor house hotels offer the ideal setting for demanding conferences, meetings and presentations. Apart from historical ambiances the participants

Tagungen, Seminare und Präsentationen. Neben historischem Ambiente finden die Teilnehmer eine moderne Ausstattung und zeitgemäße Technik vor. Kreativität und Produktivität lassen sich durch eine ansprechende und außergewöhnliche Umgebung, erstklassigen Service und ein besonderes Flair steigern. Nach vollbrachter Arbeit wird für die Gäste der „Wohlfühlfaktor" groß geschrieben: Die Angebote reichen von Ayurveda bis Thalasso und decken Beauty, Fitness, Massagen und Sport gleichermaßen ab.

can expect modern furnishings and up-to-date technology. Creativity and productivity are increased through pleasant and unique environments, first-class service and a certain panache. After the work is done, the "feel good factor" for the guests is given special attention: The possibilities range from Ayurveda to Thalasso and include beauty, gym, massages and sport. Spa and bathing facilities as well as lovingly maintained castle gardens provide the perfect surroundings in which to relax.

Wellness- und Badelandschaften sowie liebevoll gepflegte Schlossgärten laden zur Entspannung ein. Spitzenköche setzen kulinarische Akzente, für Zerstreuung sorgen u. a. zünftige Rittermahle, Tai Chi im Kloster, Floßbauen, Segeltörns auf der Ostsee und Bogenschießen im Schlosspark.

Als „Gast im Schloss" kann sich der Besucher sicher sein, wunderbare und unvergessliche Tage zu verleben. Weitere Informationen und Angebote unter

www.gast-im-schloss.de

Top professional chefs provide culinary emphasis, whilst other leisurely distractions include, amongst other things, hearty medieval banquets, Tai Chi in the monastery, raft building, sailing trips on the Baltic Sea and archery in the castle park.

As a castle guest, the visitor can rest assured that they will experience a wonderful and unforgettable time. Further information and special offers at

www.gast-im-schloss.de

German Castles
GAST IM SCHLOSS

SCHLOSS LÜTGENHOF

Gastgeberin/hostess: Katharina Stinnes-Mauch

Ulmenweg 10 · 23942 Dassow · Germany
Telefon: +49 (0) 38826-8250 · Fax: +49 (0) 38826-82522
www.schloss-luetgenhof.de
info@schloss-luetgenhof.de

Das Hotel

Am Naturschutzgebiet rund um den Dassower See liegt das klassizistische Schloss Lütgenhof. Gestaltung und Interieur der 23 Zimmer im modernen Design, verbunden mit einer warmen, wohnlichen Farbgebung, stehen durch die Anlehnung an die Deutschen Werkstätten im Kontrast zum klassizistischen Stil des Schlosses. Im Restaurant kocht Frank Schicker eine innovative Küche, inspiriert von mediterranen und regionalen mecklenburgischen Einflüssen.

The hotel

The classical Luetgenhof Castle lies on the protected landscape around the Dassow Lake. The modern design and interior of the 23 rooms combined with a warm, homely colour scheme in the style of German studios stand in contrast to the classical style of the castle. In the restaurant Frank Schicker cooks an innovative cuisine, inspired by Mediterranean and regional Mecklenburger influences.

Hotel 🛎 🛎 🛎 🛎

Restaurant 🍸 🍸 🍸 🍸

Angebot/facility

(3) 107-127 €€

(20) 129-194 €€

A/S (3) 600-720 €/week

(2) 15-40

Mo.

5 km

20/90 km

Anfahrt/journey

Bereits 1539 wurde Lütgenhof als Lehnsgut eingetragen, doch begannen die Herren von Paepcke erst 1839 mit der Errichtung des Herrenhauses. Im Zuge der Renovierung erfolgten 1890 der Umbau zum klassizistischen Schloss sowie der Anbau des Nordflügels und Wintergartens. 1945 wurde Familie von Paepcke enteignet. Das Schloss erlebte in den folgenden Jahren sehr unterschiedliche Nutzungen, bis 1992 die komplette Restaurierung begann. Um die Symmetrie der Anlage zu vervollständigen, erfolgte der Anbau des Südflügels mit Schlossterrasse, die heute mediterranes Flair unter uralten Kastanien mit einer Brise Ostseewind versprüht. Als Hotel öffnete Schloss Lütgenhof im April 1999 seine Türen und bietet heute auch einen Wellness-Bereich sowie Ferienwohnungen versteckt im Garten.

Already by 1539 Luetgenhof was registered as a fiefdom, but it was not until 1839 that the Lords of Paepcke began to build the manor house. In 1890, during the course of the renovation, it was converted to a classical castle and the north wing annex and conservatory were built. In 1945 the Paepcke family were expropriated. The castle had many different uses in the years to follow, up until the complete restoration began in 1992. In order to complete the symmetry of the annex, the extension of the south wing was built with castle terrace, which today is bursting with Mediterranean panache under ancient chestnut trees with a Baltic Sea breeze. Luetgenhof Castle opened its doors as a hotel in April 1999 and today also offers a spa as well as holiday apartments hidden in the garden.

In der näheren Umgebung:

Biosphärenreservat Schaalsee (20 km): 30.257 ha große, waldreiche Seenlandschaft in Mecklenburg-Vorpommern, mit dem Schaalsee als tiefstem See (72 m) der Norddeutschen Tiefebene; **Naturstrände in Rosenhagen und Barendorf (8 - 10 km); Lübeck (25 km):** Heinrich- und Thomas-Mann-Zentrum, Dom als erster monumentaler Backsteinbau an der Oststee, Lübeck per Kanu entdecken, Hansestadt; **Wismar (47 km):** UNESCO-Weltkulturerbe, Hansestadt, Wassertor, mittelalterliche Bürgerhäuser, Wasserkunst auf dem Marktplatz.

In the surrounding area:

Schaalsee Biosphere reservation (12 miles): 30,257 hectares of forest-rich sea-landscape in Mecklenburg-Western Pomerania, with the Schaalsee as the deepest lake (72 m) of the north German lowlands; **Nature beaches in Rosenhagen und Barendorf (5-6 miles); Lübeck (16 miles):** Heinrich and Thomas Mann centre, cathedral as the first monumental brick building on the Baltic Sea, discover Lübeck by canoe, Hanseatic city; **Wismar (29 miles):** UNESCO world cultural heritage, Hanseatic city, water gate, medieval community centres, Wasserkunst fountain on the market place.

ReiseArt Tipp!

Die Gegend rund um Dassow und der Klützer Winkel laden zum Entdecken ein, ob zu Fuß, per Fahrrad oder Auto. Eine Schlössertour im Klützer Winkel von Dassow über Grevesmühlen, einer der ältesten Orte Mecklenburgs, bis nach Lübstorf am Schweriner See bietet sich ebenso an wie eine Radtour durch den Holmer Wald. Der Dassower See lädt als eines der größten Vogelschutzgebiete Deutschlands mit über 300 Entenarten ebenso ein wie eine Stadtführung durch Dassow.

The area around Dassow and the Angle of Kluetzer (Klützer Winkel) invite you to explore by foot, bicycle or car. A tour of the castle in the Angle of Kluetzer (Klützer Winkel) of Dassow through Grevesmuehlen, one of the oldest places in Mecklenburg, to Luebstorf on the Schweriner Lake is an offer, as is a bicycle tour through the Holmer Forest. The Dassow Lake, as one of the largest bird protected areas of Germany with over 300 kinds of duck, is just as inviting as a guided tour of Dassow.

Auf den Spuren der Hanse

Der Hanse – einer Organisation von niederdeutschen Fernkaufleuten – gehörten rund 70 große und 100 bis 130 kleinere Städte an. Ihr Gebiet reichte von der niederländischen Zuidersee im Westen bis zum baltischen Estland im Osten und vom schwedischen Visby im Norden bis zur Linie Köln-Erfurt-Breslau-Krakau im Süden. Die hanseatischen Kaufleute erschlossen einen wirtschaftlichen Einflussbereich, der im 16. Jahrhundert von Portugal bis Russland und von den skandinavischen Ländern bis nach Italien reichte.

On the trail of the Hanseatic League

The Hanseatic League - an organisation of merchants within the cities of North Germany – was made up of approximately 70 large and 100 to 130 smaller cities. Its area extended from the Dutch Zuidersee in the west up to the Baltic Estonia in the east and from the Swedish Visby in the north up to the Cologne-Erfurt-Breslau-Krakau line in the south. The Hanseatic merchants developed an economic sphere of influence, that in the 16th century extended from Portugal to Russia and from the Scandinavian countries down to Italy.

Oben: Wasserkunst, Wismar
Links: Die Bark „Seute Deern“ in Bremerhaven

Above: Wasserkunst, Wismar
Left: The Bark "Seute Deern" in Bremerhaven

In ihrer Blütezeit konnte die Hanse aufgrund ihrer Machtstellung wirtschaftliche Interessen mit der Verhängung von Wirtschaftsblockaden gegen Königreiche und Fürstentümer oder mit kriegerischen Mitteln durchsetzen. Vom 13. bis in die Mitte des 15. Jahrhunderts beherrschte die Hanse weitgehend den Fernhandel des nördlichen Europas. Die Kaufleute versorgten West- und Mitteleuropa mit Luxuswaren, Nahrungsmitteln und Rohstoffen des nördlichen und östlichen Europa, wie z. B. Pelzen, Wachs, Getreide, Fisch, Flachs, Hanf und Holz. Gleichzeitig brachten sie in die Länder Nord- und Osteuropas die gewerblichen Fertigprodukte des

Oben: Universitätsplatz, Rostock
Rechts oben: Kröppeliner Straße, Rostock
Rechts unten: Fischverkauf

In its heyday, due to its powerful position, the Hanseatic League was able to assert its economic interests by imposing economic blockades against kingdoms and principalities or via military means. From the 13th until the middle of the 15th century the Hanseatic League controlled a large part of northern Europe's long-distance trade. The traders supplied western and central Europe with luxury goods, food and raw materials from northern and eastern Europe, e.g. furs, wax, cereals, fish, flax, hemp and timber. At the same time they brought the commercially finished products from the west and the south into the countries of northern and eastern Europe, e.g. cloth, metal goods, weapons

Above: University place, Rostock
Above right: Kröppeliner street, Rostock
Down right: Sale of fish

GENERALI

Westens und Südens, wie z. B. Tuche, Metallwaren, Waffen und Gewürze.

Das Stadtbild der Hanse zeichnet sich durch eine starke bauliche Geschlossenheit und regelmäßige Strukturierung aus. Eine zentrale Rolle kam dabei dem Markt zu, der eine wichtige Funktion als Treff- und Mittelpunkt innehatte. Die Gebäude in den Küstenstädten der Hanse wurden meist aus tiefroten bis hellgelben Backsteinen errichtet. Unterschiedliche Giebel und Fassaden ermöglichten eine individuelle Gestaltung der Häuser.

Im 16. und 17. Jahrhundert hatte die überregionale Handelsgemeinschaft trotz enormer Zuwächse im Handel mit der Konkurrenz der aufkommenden nationa-

Links: Rathaus, Stralsund
Oben: Stralsund, Giebelhäuser am Alten Markt, rechts das sog. Wulflamhaus

and spices. The cityscape of the Hanseatic League is characterised by a strong architectural uniformity and regular structuring. The market held an important function, a central role, as a meeting and a focal point. The buildings in the coastal towns of the Hanseatic League were usually built from deep red to light yellow bricks. Different gables and facades produced houses with an individual design.

In the 16th and 17th centuries the national trading community, in spite of enormous increases in trade, had to fight competition in the form of the emerging national and territorial endeavours. It increasingly continued to lose more importance in the time that followed. In Luebeck the last

Left: Cityhall, Stralsund
Above: Stralsund, gabled houses at the old market place right the 'Wulflamhaus'

len und territorialen Bestrebungen zu kämpfen. Sie verlor in der Folgezeit immer mehr an Bedeutung. In Lübeck fand im Jahre 1669 der letzte Hansetag statt.
Lübeck: Lübeck war das einstige Haupt der Hanse, seinen Aufstieg verdankte es in erster Linie seiner herausragenden verkehrsgeographischen Lage. Die von der Ostsee kommenden Schiffe konnten über die Trave bis in den Stadthafen fahren. Das doppeltürmige Holstentor der mittelalterlichen Stadtbefestigung ist seit 1478 das Wahrzeichen der Stadt.
Wismar: Das schöne mittelalterliche Stadtbild, das weitgehend bewahrt werden konnte, begeistert auch heute

Hanseatic day took place in the year 1669.
Luebeck: Luebeck was the former head of the Hanseatic League, its ascent was owed primarily to its outstanding geographical position for transport. The ships coming from the Baltic Sea could travel across the Trave River into the town port. The Holsten Gate with its two towers forms part of the medieval town's fortification and has been its landmark since 1478.
Wismar: The beautiful medieval townscape, which to a large extent was able to be preserved, continues to elate visitors from all over the world. The market place

Links oben: Holstentor zu Lübeck
Links unten: Luftbild der Hansestadt Lübeck
Oben: ehem. Lotsenstation, das Segelschiff „Gorch Fock“ (nicht zu verwechseln mit der „Gorch Fock“ der Bundesmarine), Wismar

Above left: Holsten Gate, Luebeck
Down left: Aerial view over Hanseatic town Luebeck
Above: Former Guide Station, Sailing Ship “Gorch Fock” (no to mistake it for the “Gorch Fock” of the Federal marine), Wismar

Besucher aus aller Welt. Der Marktplatz mit seinen beeindruckenden historischen Bauten, dient von jeher als Treff- und Mittelpunkt der Stadt.

Rostock: Bedeutende Stadt der Hanse; die eindrucksvollen Backsteinfassaden, die Giebelhäuser und mächtigen Kirchen im Stadtzentrum zeugen noch heute vom einstigen Reichtum der Kaufleute.

Stralsund: Die Hansestadt gehört heute zum UNESCO-Weltkulturerbe. Restaurierte Bürgerhäuser und imposante Backsteinkirchen sowie die Einzigartigkeit des gesamten Stadtensembles gehören zu den wertvollen Zeugnissen der Hansezeit.

with its impressive historical buildings, has always served as a meeting and focal point of the town.

Rostock: Important city of the Hanseatic League; the impressive brick fronts, the gable houses and mighty churches in the town centre still stand witness today of the former wealth of the traders.

Stralsund: The Hanseatic town today belongs to UNESCO world cultural heritage. Restored town houses and impressive brick churches as well as the uniqueness of the entire town form part of the valuable reference points to the Hanseatic time.

Oben: Blick auf Stralsund
Rechts: Gorch Fock I, Stralsund.; Zur Kogge, Rostock; Nikolaikirche, Wismar; St. Jakobi, Stralsund

Above: View over Stralsund
Right: Gorch Fock I, Stalsund.; Zur Kogge, Rostock; Church St. Niclas, Wismar; St. Jakobi, Stralsund

Herr, ich habe
lieb die Stätte Deines
Hauses und den Ort,
da Deine Ehre
wohnet.
Ps. 26 V. 8

German Castles
GAST IM SCHLOSS

BURGHOTEL BLOMBERG

Gastgeberin/hostess: Ines Claus

Burg 1 · 32825 Blomberg · Germany
Telefon: +49 (0) 5235-50010 · Fax: +49 (0) 5235-500145
www.burghotel-blomberg.de
info@burghotel-blomberg.de

Das Hotel

Direkt am Teutoburger Wald erwarten stilvoll gestaltete Zimmer, exklusive Themen-Suiten, eine Weinberg- und eine Sonnenterrasse die Gäste zu allen Jahreszeiten. Neben kirchlichen Hochzeiten in der hauseigenen Christuskapelle können auch standesamtliche Trauungen durchgeführt werden. Im Restaurant verspricht der Kamin knisternde Atmosphäre. Als kulinarisches Erlebnis der besonderen Art steht der Gewölbekeller für Rittergelage zur Verfügung.

The hotel

Directly on the edge of the Teutoburger Forest, stylishly designed rooms, exclusive themed suites, a vineyard and a sun terrace await the guests in all seasons. Apart from church weddings in the hotel's own Christ Chapel, civil marriage ceremonies can also be arranged. In the restaurant, the fireplace promises crackling ambiances. For special culinary experiences, the vault cellar is available for knightly banquets.

Hotel

Restaurant

Angebot/facility

(6) 84-105 €€

(42) 100-190 €€

A/S (5) 300-500 €€

(11) 4-250

3 km

49/86 km

Anfahrt/journey

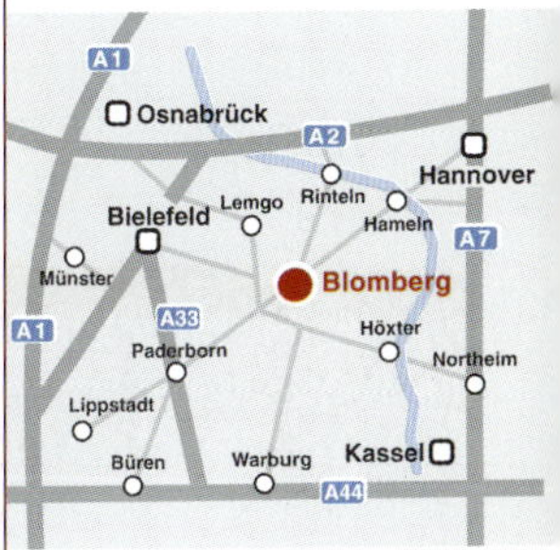

Historisch zurückverfolgen lässt sich die Geschichte der Burg Blomberg bis in die Zeit zwischen 1231 und 1255. Spätgotische Einflüsse, als auch Einflüsse der Renaissance sind gut zu erkennen. 1567 entstand zunächst im spätgotischen Stil der zweistöckige Nordflügel, der zum Innenhof als Fachwerkbau errichtet wurde. Das Mittelhaus mit dem Fachwerkobergeschoss und seinen prachtvollen Schnitzereien im Renaissance-Stil wurde 1569 erbaut. Der Ostflügel beeindruckt durch einen zweigeschossigen Erker im klassischen Renaissance-Stil. Die Burg ist seit 1962 im Besitz der Stadt Blomberg. Seit 1974 wird darin ein Hotel betrieben.

The Blomberg Castle lets itself go historically back in time to the period between 1231 and 1255. Late gothic influences as well as Renaissance influences are easy to recognize. In 1567 the two-storey north wing was initially built in the late gothic style in the inner courtyard as a timber building. The central house, with the timber construction upper floor and its grand carvings in the Renaissance style, was built in 1569. The east wing is impressive thanks to its two-storey high oriel in the classical Renaissance style. The town of Blomberg has owned the castle since 1962. Since 1974 a hotel has been run inside the castle.

In der näheren Umgebung:
Hameln (35 km): Rattenfänger-Museum; **Detmold (18 km):** Residenzschloss mit Führungen; Freilichtmuseum bäuerlicher Kulturdenkmale; Adlerwarte Berlebeck mit der ältesten Greifvogelwarte Europas; Hermannsdenkmal auf der 386 m hohen Grotenburg, dichtes Netz an Wanderwegen; **Schieder (3 km):** Erholungszentrum Emmerstausee mit 90 qm großem Stausee, Rundwanderwegen, Möglichkeiten zum Segeln, Surfen, Rudern, Boot- und Tretbootverleih, Rundfahrten auf dem Stausee.

In the surrounding area:
Hamelin (22 miles): The Pied Piper Museum; **Detmold (11 miles):** Residential palace with guided tours; open air museum of rural culture monuments; Berlebeck eagle look-out with the oldest raptor look-out in Europe; Hermann's monument on the 386m high Grotenburg Castle, a large network of footpaths **Schieder (2 miles):** Emmerstausee leisure centre with 90 m^2 artificial lake, circular walks, possibilities to sail, surf and row plus boat and pedalo hire, round trips on artificial lake.

ReiseArt Tipp!

Das Burghotel Blomberg ist ein idealer Ausgangspunkt für alle golfinteressierten Gäste.
Angeboten wird ein dreitägiges Golfarrangement „Golf Total" von April bis November. Golfen kann man sowohl im lippischen Golfclub in Blomberg/Cappel, dessen harmonische Anlage eine 1.000jährige Eiche, Bachläufe und Lichtungen im Hochwald umfasst, als auch in einem der anderen 16 Golfclubs der Umgebung.

The Blomberg Castle Hotel is an ideal starting point for all guests interested in golf. Special offers include a three-day-long golf programme "Golf Total" from April to November. You can play golf both in the Lippian golf club in Blomberg/Cappel, whose harmonious location covers a 1000 year old oak tree, streams and clearings in the timber forest, and in one of the other 16 golf clubs in the area.

German Castles
GAST IM SCHLOSS

DORNRÖSCHENSCHLOSS SABABURG

Gastgeber/host: Fam. Koseck

Im Reinhardswald · 34369 Hofgeismar-Sababurg · Germany
Telefon: +49 (0) 5671-8080 · Fax: +49 (0) 5671-808200
www.sababurg.de
dornroeschenschloss@sababurg.de

Das Hotel

Umgeben von wild-romantischen Rosengärten, Rosenhecken und Rosensträuchern steht mitten im Reinhardswald die Sababurg. Dass Rosen hier eine bedeutende Rolle spielen, zeigen auch der hauseigene Rosenlikör sowie die eigene Sababurg-Rose.

Das Himmelbett im Turmzimmer lädt zu einer Reise in die märchenhafte Vergangenheit ein. Im Restaurant warten auf den Gast hessische Spezialitäten, die auf sehr angenehme Weise neu interpretiert werden.

The hotel

Surrounded by wild romantic rose gardens, rose hedges and rose bushes, Sababurg lies in the heart of the Reinhards Forest. The hotel's own rose liquor as well as the Sababurg Rose reflect the important role that the rose plays here.

The four-poster bed in the tower room invites you on a journey into the fairytale past. Hessian specialities await the guest in the restaurant, which have been newly interpreted in very appetising ways.

Hotel 🛎 🛎 🛎

Restaurant 🍸 🍸 🍸 🍸

Angebot/facility

(17) 145-205 €€

(3) bis 40

12 km

25 km

Anfahrt/journey

Bereits 1334 wurde die „Zappenborgk" gebaut und diente den Pilgern des nahen Wallfahrtsortes als Schutz. Nachdem das Schloss in den folgenden Jahrhunderten verfiel, wurde es später zum Jagdschloss umgebaut. Heute erinnern die nach den ursprünglichen Tiernamen benannten Zimmer an diese Zeit. Als einer der ersten in Europa gründete Wilhelm IV. 1571 den 130 ha großen Tierpark, der nicht nur als Jagdrevier, sondern auch als Ort der Forschung diente. Unter Landgraf Moritz von Hessen fanden im 17. Jahrhundert die ersten Theateraufführungen statt. Heute ist das kleine Ensemble des Sababurg-Theaters fester Bestandteil des Dornröschenschlosses. 1959 wurde das Schloss zum Hotel umgebaut und wird seitdem liebevoll von Familie Koseck geführt.

The "Zappenborgk" had already been built by 1334 and served as a shelter for the pilgrims of the nearby place of pilgrimage. As the castle became derelict over the centuries to come it was later converted into a hunting lodge. Today the rooms, named after the original animal names, are a reminder of this time. As one of the first in Europe, in 1571 William IV. established the 130 hectares zoo, which not only served as hunting ground but also as a place for research. Under the State Count Moritz of Hessen in the 17th century, the first theatre performances took place. Today the small ensemble of the Sababurg Theatre is an integral part of the Sleeping Beauty Castle. In 1959 the castle was converted into the hotel and has since then been lovingly run by the Koseck family.

In der näheren Umgebung:
Sababurg: Tierpark mit Greifvogelstation sowie Forst- und Jagdmuseum; **Hofgeismar:** Apothekenmuseum im 900 Jahre alten „Steinernen Haus"; **Kassel:** Bergpark und Habichtswald Wilhelmshöhe – mit 300 ha Europas größter Bergpark, über 600 verschiedene Gehölzarten, Herkules, Wasserkünste, Schloss und andere Sehenswürdigkeiten; Brüder-Grimm Museum und Archiv im Palais Bellevue.

In the surrounding area
Sababurg: Zoo with raptor point as well as a forest and hunting museum; **Hofgeismar:** Pharmacy Museum in the 900 year old "Steinernen Haus" (stone house); **Kassel:** Mountain park and Habichtswald Wilhelmshöhe – Europe's largest mountain park with 300 hectares, over 600 different kinds of trees, Hercules statue, water features, castle and other points of interest; the Brothers Grimm Museum and archives in the Bellevue Palace.

ReiseArt Tipp!

In der „documenta-Stadt" Kassel findet vom 1. September bis 20. November 2005 in der Kunsthalle Fridericianum die Ausstellung „50 Jahre documenta 1955 - 2005" statt. Anhand eines archivarischen, kunsthistorischen, ortsspezifischen, filmischen sowie wissenschaftlichen Kapitels wird aus heutiger Perspektive die von Widersprüchen und Brüchen gekennzeichnete Entwicklung der *documenta* betrachtet.

In the "Documenta Town" Kassel from 1st September to 20th November 2005 the exhibition "50 years documenta 1955 - 2005" will take place in the Fridericianum Art Gallery. Based on an archival, art historical, site-specific, cinematic as well as scientific chapter, the *documenta* is reconsidered from today's perspective of development marked by contradictions and inconsistencies.

Auf den Spuren der Märchenerzähler

Wer kennt sie nicht die Brüder Jacob und Wilhelm Grimm. Als Sprachforscher sammelten und veröffentlichten sie Märchen und Sagen und entwickelten die Grundzüge einer Grammatik.
Zwischen ihrem Geburtsort Hanau, östlich von Frankfurt gelegen, und Bremen, wo ihnen mit den „Bremer Stadtmusikanten" ein Denkmal gesetzt wurde, verläuft die Deutsche Märchenstraße.
Durch reizvolle Flusstäler und Mittelgebirgslandschaften, vorbei an Burgen und Schlössern, durch mittelalterliche, verwinkelte Fachwerkstädtchen führt die Märchenstraße nicht nur zu den Wirkungsstätten der Brüder Grimm (Hanau, Steinau, Marburg, Kassel und Göttingen), sondern auch zu Schauplätzen einiger berühmter Märchen (Dornröschenschloss Sababurg oder Frau-Holle-Teich auf dem Hohen Meißner). In der malerischen alten Universitätsstadt Marburg begannen die Brüder Grimm ihre Forschungen.
Zwischen Marburg und Fritzlar liegt das Rotkäppchenland. Die mittelalterli-

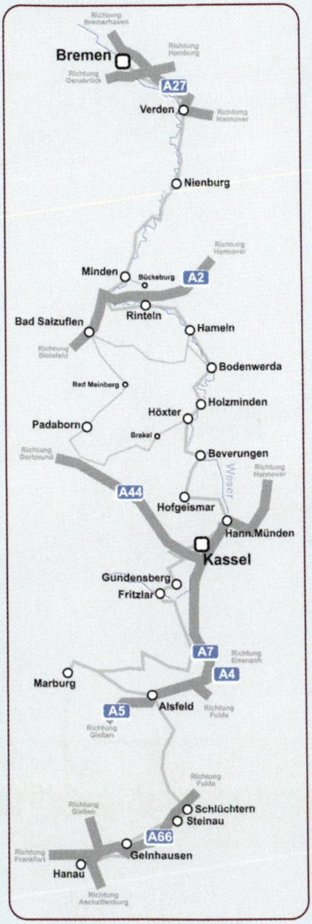

On the trail of the fairytale storytellers

Who has not heard of the brothers Jacob and William Grimm. As linguists they collected and published fairy tales and legends and developed the fundamentals of grammar. The German Fairytale Road runs between their place of birth Hanau, east of Frankfurt, and Bremen, where their "Bremen musicians" monument is set.
Through delightful river valleys and low mountain range landscapes, past castles, through medieval, small, winding, half-timbered towns, the Fairytale Road leads not only to the places of work of the Brothers Grimm (Hanau, Steinau, Marburg, Kassel and Goettingen), but also to the settings of some famous fairy tales (Sababurg Sleeping Beauty Castle or Mother Holle Pond on the Hohe Meißner Hill). The picturesque old university town of Marburg is where the Brothers Grimm began their research.
Red Riding Hood country lies between Marburg and Fritzlar. The medieval cathedral and imperial town of Fritzlar is still nearly completely surrounded by the town wall with towers.

Links: Die Bremer Stadtmusikanten

Left: Bremen musicians

che Dom- und Kaiserstadt Fritzlar ist noch fast vollständig von einer mit Türmen gespickten Stadtmauer umgeben. Unterwegs auf der Märchenstraße erschließen sich noch andere Orte berühmter Geschichten und Überlieferungen, wie die des Rattenfängers von Hameln oder des Baron Münchhausen in Bodenwerder an der mittleren Weser.
Schloss und Park Wilhelmshöhe erinnern in Kassel an die Bedeutung der Stadt zur Renaissance- und Barockzeit. Die pittoreske Löwenburg – außen bröckelnde Burgruine, innen wohnliche Sommerresidenz – von Kurfürst Wilhelm erbaut, bot schon zu Zeiten der Brüder Grimm eine märchenhafte Kulisse. Im Palais

Continuing along the Fairytale Road other places of famous stories and traditions are revealed, like that of the Pied Piper of Hamlin or Baron Muenchhausen in Bodenwerder on the middle Weser.
Wilhelmshoehe Castle and Park serve as reminders in Kassel of the significance of the city in Renaissance and Baroque times. The picturesque Lion Castle – on the outside a crumbling castle ruin, inside a homely summer residence – built by the Elector William, provided from time to time a fairytale setting for the Brothers Grimm. The Bellevue Palace houses the Brothers Grimm Museum as well as the Grimm archives and library. The Fridericianum Arts Centre is the headquarter of the re-

Oben: Schloss Marburg

Above: Castle Marburg

Bellevue sind das Brüder Grimm Museum sowie Grimm-Archiv und -Bibliothek beherbergt. Die Kunsthalle Fridericianum ist Hauptsitz der renommierten, alle vier Jahre stattfindenden „documenta".
Nicht weit von Kassel entfernt liegt das Märchenland Reinhardswald und darin die Sababurg mit Rosengarten und Wildpark, die als Dornröschenschloss der Brüder Grimm gilt.
Im Park Gesundbrunnen erinnern Badehäuser und Brunnentempel an die Blütezeit des alten Heilbades Hofgeismar.
Hameln lädt mit seinen schönen alten Bürgerhäusern zum Stadtrundgang auf der „Rattenspur", ganz im Zeichen der weltberühmten Rattenfängersage ein.

nowned, "documenta" that takes place every 4 years. Not far from Kassel is the Fairytale country Reinhards Forest in which lies the Sababurg Castle with rose garden and wild animal park, considered the Sleeping Beauty Castle of the Brothers Grimm.
In the Gesundbrunnen Park the bath houses and well temples serve as reminders of the heyday of the old Hofgeismar therapeutic bath.
With its beautiful old town houses Hamlin invites you on a tour of the town following the "trail of the rats", just as is told in the world-famous Pied Piper legend. The starting point is in the town centre at the Pferdemarkt (horse market).

Links: Schlösschen Bellvue, Kassel
Rechts oben: Fridericianum, Kassel
Rechts unten: documenta-Halle, Kassel

Left: Castle Bellvue, Kassel
Above right: Fridericianum, Kassel
Down right: documenta-hall, Kassel

Start ist im Zentrum auf dem Pferdemarkt. In der Nähe der Stadt Horn geht es über den „Hermannsweg" zu den Externsteinen: einem sagenumwobenen Natur- und Kulturdenkmal aus vorchristlicher Zeit, das bereits von Goethe bewundert wurde. In der Nähe erhebt sich bei Detmold das Hermannsdenkmal, das an die Schlacht im Teutoburger Wald (9 n. Chr.) erinnert, in der das römische Heer vom Cheruskerfürsten Arminius vernichtend geschlagen wurde.

Von Bückeburg, einem Juwel der Weserrenaissance, geht es über Minden, Nienburg und Verden an der Weser entlang bis in die alte Hansestadt Bremen, die mit vielen interessanten Gebäuden und Museen aufwarten kann. Die „Bremer

Links: Rattenfängerhaus, Hameln
Rechts: Brüder Gimm Denkmal, Kassel

Near the town of Horn the route runs along "Hermanns Path" to the Extern stones: a legendary natural and cultural monument from pre-Christian times, which was admired by Goethe. Nearby at Detmold is where Hermanns Monument stands, commemorating the battle in the Teutoburger Forest (9 AD), in which the Roman army was crushingly defeated by Arminius, the Prince of Cherusci.

From Bueckeburg, a gem of the Weser Renaissance, the route continues through Minden, Nienburg and Verden on the River Weser until the old Hanseatic town of Bremen, with many interesting buildings and museums to be seen. The "Bremen musicians" monu-

Left: House of Pied Piper of Hamelin
Right: Monument "Brothers Grimm", Kassel

Stadtmusikanten“ an der Westseite des Rathauses, gelten als das bekannteste Denkmal der Stadt.
Die Böttcherstraße, eine 110 m lange Passage, in der die Böttcher früher ihre Fässer fertigten, wurde in den Jahren 1924 bis 1931 von Bernhard Hoettger, einem Mitbegründer der Darmstädter

ment to the west side of the town hall, is considered as the most well-known monument of the city.
The ‘Boettcherstrasse’ (Cooper Street), a 110 m long passage, in which the coopers formerly produced their barrels, was expressionistically transformed in 1924 to 1931 by Bernhard Hoettger, a

Oben: Externsteine

Above: Extern-stones

Künstlerkolonie, expressionistisch umgestaltet (siehe „Auf den Spuren des Jugendstils“ Seite 115).
Nur 25 km von Bremen entfernt liegt die Künstlerkolonie Worpswede, ebenfalls mit vielen Bauten Bernhard Hoettgers.

co-founder of the Darmstaedt artists' colony. (See “On the trail of art nouveau” page 112).
Only 15 miles away from Bremen is the Worpswede artists' colony, which also has many Bernhard Hoettger buildings.

Oben: Böttcherstraße und Kunsthalle, Bremen
Unten: Neues Museum Weserburg, Bremen
Rechts oben: Barkenhof in Worpswede
Rechts unten: Paula Moderson-Becker Museum

Above: Street Böttcher and Arthall, Bremen
Down: New Museum Weserburg, Bremen
Above right: Barkenhof in Worpswede
Down right: Paula Moderson-Becker Museum

German Castles
GAST IM SCHLOSS

SCHLOSS WALDECK

Gastgeber/host: Karl F. Isenberg

34513 Waldeck am Edersee · Germany
Telefon: +49 (0) 5623-5890 · Fax: +49 (0) 5623-589289
www.schloss-waldeck.de
schlosswaldeck@aol.com

Das Hotel

Das auf einem Felsen erbaute Schloss Waldeck thront 200 m über dem 27 km langen Edersee. Alle Zimmer des Schlosshotels gewähren einen unvergesslichen Panoramablick über das Waldecker Land und den Edersee. Zum Haus gehören neben zahlreichen Salons und Sälen auch das Restaurant „Alte Turmuhr", die Hotelbar im „Gesindekeller" sowie das Panoramarestaurant, Sauna, Schwimmbad und Poolwiese.

The hotel

The Waldeck Castle built on a rock towers 200m over the 17 mile long Eder Lake. All rooms of the Castle Hotel grant an unforgettable panoramic view over the Waldeck countryside and the Eder Lake. In addition to numerous salons and halls, the hotel also has the "Old Tower Clock" Restaurant, the hotel bar in the "servants' cellar", as well as the panoramic restaurant, sauna, swimming pool and adjoining lawn.

Hotel 🛎🛎🛎🛎

Restaurant 🍸🍸🍸🍸

Angebot/facility

(1) 98-153 €€

(35) 146-162 €€

A/S (4) 198-207 €€

(9) bis 260

3.1.-15.2.

42 km

75/210 km

Anfahrt/journey

Vom 11. bis ins 18. Jahrhundert war Waldeck als Stammburg der Grafen von Waldeck auch Regierungssitz. Mit Erlangung der Fürstenwürde zogen die Grafen um in das neue Schloss Arolsen. Waldeck wurde nun Landeshauptarchiv, Zeughaus, Landeszuchthaus sowie Fürstliches Hauptforstamt, bevor es die heutige Bestimmung als Schlosshotel fand.

Bei Burgführungen durch die Verliese, die Gewölbe und den 120 m tiefen Brunnen erlebt man die ereignisreichen Jahrhunderte der Burg. Aus der Zeit des Landeszuchthauses berichtet das Museum unter dem Titel „Hinter Schloss und Riegel".

From the 11th up to the 18th century, Waldeck was, as the family seat of the Counts of Waldeck, also the seat of government. Having acquired the titular dignities of Prince, the Counts moved to the new Arolsen Castle. Waldeck then became the main national archive, an armoury, national jail, as well as the royal forestry head office, before adopting its present day purpose as a castle hotel.

The eventful centuries of castle history are to be experienced on a guided tour of the castle through the dungeons, vaults and the 120 m deep well. From the time dating back to the national jail, the museum reports with the caption "under lock and key".

In der näheren Umgebung:
Schloss Waldeck: Burgmuseum, Besichtigung der Verliese, Panoramaterrassen; **Nationalpark und Naturpark Kellerwald-Edersee:** Buchennationalpark, Wildpark mit Greifvogelflugshow, Nationalpark-Wanderungen mit Ranger, **Edersee/Staumauer:** Einer der größten deutschen Stauseen (202 Mio. m^{33} Wasser), Radwanderwege (63 km), alle Wassersportarten möglich; **Schloss Arolsen:** Neue fürstliche Residenz, Museen, Schlossführungen.

In the surrounding area:
Waldeck Castle: Castle museum, tour of the dungeons, panoramic terraces; **National park and Keller Forest and Eder Lake Nature Park:** Beech national park, game park with raptor show, national park walking tours with the ranger; **Eder Lake/concrete dam:** One of Germany's large reservoirs (202 million m^3 of water), cycle paths (39 miles), all watersports available; Arolsen Castle: New royal residence, Museums, guided tours of the castle.

ReiseArt Tipp!

Einen Ausflug wert ist das moderne Heilbäder-Zentrum Bad Wildungen. In der 1200 Jahre alten heutigen Kurstadt kann man sich in den Heilbädern und Kurparks erholen. Interessierte finden im Kurmuseum nicht nur die Geschichte der Kur- und Badeanstalten, sondern auch eine im Keller sprudelnde Quelle.
Im Besucherbergwerk Bertsch kann man zu den Bergleuten des Mittelalters hinabsteigen.

The modern therapeutic bath centre in Bad Wildungen is well worth a visit. The present day 1200 year old spa town is a place for relaxation with therapeutic baths and spa gardens. Those interested in paying a visit to the spa museum will not only find the history of the spa homes and baths, but also a gushing wellspring in the cellar. In the Bertsch visitors' mine you can go down to see the miners of the Middle Ages.

German Castles
GAST IM SCHLOSS

SCHLOSS SPANGENBERG

Gastgeber/host: Fam. Wichmann

Schloss 1 · 34286 Spangenberg · Germany
Telefon: +49 (0) 5663-93980 · Fax: +49 (0) 5663-7567
www.schloss-spangenberg.de
info@schloss-spangenberg.de

Das Hotel

Im reizvollen Seitental der Fulda, inmitten des Kurhessischen Berglandes, befindet sich Schloss Spangenberg, das mit seinem Burggraben, der hölzernen Zugbrücke und den Torhäusern allen Vorstellungen von einer alten Burganlage gerecht wird. Die stilvoll gestalteten Zimmer sind komfortabel und geräumig. Zum Haus gehören auch eine eigene Konditorei sowie das Restaurant mit einer internationalen, leichten Küche, die als besondere Spezialität Wildgerichte anbietet.

The hotel

In a delightful side valley of the River Fulda and in the midst of Hessian spa mountain landscape lies Spangenberg Castle, which with its castle moat, wooden drawbridge and gatekeeper's cabin lives up to all traditional expectations of an old castle. The stylishly furnished rooms are comfortable and spacious. The hotel also has its own pastry shop on the premises as well as a restaurant with an international, light cuisine, offering game dishes as a particular speciality.

Hotel 🛎 🛎 🛎

Restaurant 🍸 🍸 🍸

Angebot/facility

- (4) 45-96 €
- (20) 99-158 €€
- A/S (1) 183 €€
- (2) -150
- 12 km
- 200 km

Anfahrt/journey

Die im 13. Jahrhundert erbaute Burganlage diente anfangs dem Schutz der Handelsstraße vom Rhein-Main-Gebiet nach Leipzig. Nach dem Verkauf an den hessischen Landgrafen Heinrich II. im Jahre 1350 wurde die Burg als Jagd- und Lustschloss genutzt. Trotz der im 30jährigen Krieg verstärkten Befestigungsmauern wurde Schloss Spangenberg 1758 kurzfristig von den Franzosen erobert. Während der folgenden Jahrhunderte wurde die Burg vielfältig genutzt: als preußische Forstschule, als Gefangenenlager im Krieg gegen Frankreich 1870/71 und im Zweiten Weltkrieg. 1945 wurde die Festung zerstört, ab 1950 jedoch wieder aufgebaut. Wieder hergestellt wurde auch der Schlossbrunnen, der mit 105 m fast seine ursprüngliche Tiefe von 128 m erreicht.

The 13th century castle served initially to protect the trade route from the Rhine-Main region to Leipzig. After being sold to the Hessian Landgrave Heinrich II in 1350, the castle was used as a hunting lodge and summer residence. Despite the fortified walls strengthened during the Thirty Years War, Spangenberg Castle was conquered by the French for a short time in 1758. During the centuries to follow the castle was used for various purposes: as a Prussian school of forestry and as a prison camp in the war against France in 1870/71 and in the Second World War. In 1945 the fortress was destroyed, but was rebuilt from 1950. The castle well was also restored, which with a depth of 105 m nearly achieves the original depth of 128m.

In der näheren Umgebung:
Spangenberg: Jagd- und Schlossmuseum im ehemaligen Zeughaus des Schlosses, Altstadt mit historischen Fachwerkhäusern, Marktplatzbrunnen, Stadtkirche St. Johannes der Täufer aus dem 13. bis 15. Jh., Stadtbefestigung mit Stadtmauer und Wehrtürmen (der einzige noch vollständig erhaltene und begehbare Wehrturm ist der Eulenturm); **Hoher Meißner (ca. 20 km):** 750 üNN lädt ein gut ausgebautes Wegenetz zum Wandern ein, im Winter ist auch Skilanglauf möglich.

In the surrounding area:
Spangenberg: Hunting and castle museum in the former armoury of the castle, old part of town with historical half-timbered houses, market place well, St. John the Baptist town church from the 13th to 15th centuries, town fortification with town wall and defence towers (the only still completely preserved and accessible defence tower is the Owl Tower); **Hoher Meißner (approx. 12 miles):** 750 m above sea level an extensive network of footpaths is an ideal location for walks, in the winter it is also possible to go cross-country skiing.

ReiseArt Tipp!

Auf einer Länge von rund 70 km erstreckt sich entlang des Fernwanderweges X 8 (Barbarossaweg) der Kunstpfad *Ars Natura.* Die von regionalen, überregionalen und internationalen Künstlern geschaffenen Kunstwerke haben ortsbezogenen, historischen und kulturellen Charakter. Die aus weitestgehend ökologischen Materialien geschaffenen Kunstwerke fügen sich harmonisch in die spezifische, landschaftliche Umgebung ein.

The artistic path 'Ars Natura' extends along a stretch of approx. 43 miles of the footpath marked 'X 8' (Barbarossa Path). The works of art created by regional, national and international artists have a locally orientated, historical and cultural nature. Created using for the most part ecological materials, the works of art blend harmoniously into the characteristic and scenic surroundings.

German Castles
GAST IM SCHLOSS

PARKHOTEL WASSERBURG ANHOLT

Gastgeber/hosts: Peter & Jörg Brune

Klever Straße · 46419 Isselburg · Germany
Telefon: +49 (0) 2874-4590 · Fax: +49 (0) 2874-4035
www.parkhotel-wasserburg-anholt.de
rezeption@schloss-anholt.de

Das Hotel

Die historische Burganlage, die eindrucksvolle Parklandschaft und das unverwechselbare Ambiente machen das Parkhotel Wasserburg Anholt zu einem ganz besonderen Ort der Gastlichkeit. Einzigartig sind das gläserne Restaurant mit kreativer Spitzenküche im Wasserpavillon inmitten des Wassergrabens, die Terrasse über dem Burggraben, das Standesamt sowie die individuell, mit stilvollem Luxus eingerichteten Zimmer und Salons.

The hotel

The historic site of the castle, the impressive park landscape and the unmistakable ambiance make the Anholt Moated Castle Park Hotel a very special place for hospitality. The glass restaurant with creative state-of-the-art kitchen in a water pavilion in the midst of the moat, the terrace over the castle moat, the registry office as well as the individual, stylishly luxurious furnished room and parlour are all very unique.

Hotel 4

Restaurant 4

Angebot/facility

(7) 60-89 €€

(20) 125-160 €€

A/S (6) 180-280 €€

(7) 50-124

3 km

80 km

Anfahrt/journey

Wasserburg Anholt ist von mehreren Barockgärten umgeben und liegt inmitten einer riesigen Gräfte, eingebettet in eine 42 ha große Parkanlage. Bereits seit 1645 befindet sich Anholt im Besitz der Fürsten zu Salm. Im Zweiten Weltkrieg erlitt die Anlage schwere Zerstörungen, wodurch das dauerhafte Bewohnen nicht mehr möglich war. Im Rahmen des Wiederaufbaus erhielt die Wasserburg eine museale Bestimmung. Von 1990 bis 2000 führte Fürst Carl Philipp zu Salm-Salm eingehende Wiederherstellungs- und Restaurierungsmaßnahmen historischer Räumlichkeiten sowie zahlreicher bedeutender Kunstgegenstände zur Erschließung und Einrichtung des Museums durch.

Anholt Moated Castle is surrounded by several baroque gardens and lies amidst an enormous moat, nestled in 42 hectares of parkland. The Princes of Salm have owned Anholt since 1645. In the Second World War the site was almost completely destroyed, to the extent that it was no longer inhabitable. As part of its reconstruction, the moated castle was preserved to become a museum. Between 1990 and 2000 Prince Carl Philipp of Salm-Salm carried out reconstruction and restoration measures on the historical premises, as well as on numerous important pieces of art for the development and furnishing of the museum.

In der näheren Umgebung:
Anholter Schweiz: Biotop-Wildpark mit großem Wildgehege und Fasanerie, sog. Nachahmung des Vierwaldstädter Sees
Isselburg: Hochseilgarten; **Kleve (29 km):** Kunstsammlungen im Kurhaus; **Schloss Moyland (30 km):** Museum mit Joseph Beuys Archiv (www.moyland.de); **Xanten (30 km):** Archäologischer Park Kanutouren auf der Issel, Touren mit dem Auto oder Fahrrad durch das Münsterland 2 km bis zur niederländischen Grenze.

In the surrounding area:
Anholt Switzerland: Biotope-wildlife Park with big game reserve and pheasantry, which is an imitation of the Vierwaldstädter Lakes.; **Isselburg:** High rope garden; **Kleve (18 miles):** Art collection in a spa hotel.; **Moyland Castle (19 miles):** Museum with Joseph Beuys archive (www.moyland.de); **Xanten (19 miles):** Archaeological Park: Canoeing trips on the River Issel, car drives or bicycle rides through Münster country 2 km to the Dutch border.

ReiseArt Tipp!

Museum Wasserburg Anholt: größte, historisch gewachsene Privatsammlung Nordrhein-Westfalens mit über 700 Gemälden von Rembrandt, J. Brueghel d. J., Holbein u.a.
Het Nationale Park De Hoge Veluwe: Nationalpark mit Möglichkeit ausgedehnter Fahrradtouren durch eine abwechslungsreiche Landschaft, Kröller-Müller-Museum mit Werken von van Gogh, Picasso u.a., Skulpturengarten (Fahrradverleih vor Ort).

Anholt Moated Castle Museum: the biggest, historically grown private collection in North Rhine-Westphalia with over 700 paintings by Rembrandt, J. Brueghel II and Holbein amongst others.
Het Nationale Park De Hoge Veluwe: National Park with the possibility of extensive cycle rides through varied landscapes, the Kroeller Mueller Museum with works by van Gogh, Picasso and others, sculpture garden (local bicycle rental).

Auf den Spuren großer Kunstsammlungen

Ausgangspunkt ist die Wasserburg Anholt mit der größten, historisch gewachsenen, privaten Bildersammlung Nordrhein-Westfalens. Zu besichtigen sind über 700 herausragende Arbeiten niederländischer Maler des 17. Jahrhunderts (Rembrandt, Jan van Goyen, Gerard ter Boch), flämischer (J. Brueghel d. J.), deutscher (Bartholomäus Bruyn, Holbein, Jobst Harich), spanischer (Murillo) und italienischer (Carlo Dolci, Salvator Rosa) Meister. Von Anholt aus lassen sich eine Reihe weiterer bedeutender Sammlungen erschließen.

On the trail of large art collections

The starting point is the Anholt Moated Castle with the largest, historically grown, private picture collection in North Rhine-Westphalia. There are over 700 outstanding pieces of work to be seen by 17th century Dutch painters (Rembrandt, Jan van Goyen, Gerard ter Boch), Flemish (J. Brueghel II), German (Bartholomaeus Bruyn, Holbein, Jobst Harich), Spanish (Murillo) and Italian (Carlo Dolci, Salvator Rosa) master craftsmen. From Anholt a number of further important collections are revealed.

Links: Museum Wasserburg Anholt
Oben: DER ALCHEMIST von David Teniers der Jüngere (1610-1690)

Left: Museum Wasserburg Anholt
Above: THE ALCHIMIST of David Teniers the Younger (1610-1690)

Im Het Nationale Park De Hoge Veluwe erwartet das Kröller-Müller-Museum mit seiner umfangreichen Werk-Sammlung von van Gogh, Seurat, Picasso, Léger, Mondrian und vielen anderen Künstlern der klassischen Moderne die Besucher. Die Stifterin, Helene Kröller-Müller, war die kunstinteressierte Tochter eines deutschen Industriellen und heiratete 1888 den Holländer Kröller.

Zum Museum gehört einer der größten Skulpturengärten der Welt. Er zeigt auf einer Fläche von 25 ha eine Vielzahl an Skulpturen namhafter Künstler des 20. Jahrhunderts.

Im Schloss Moyland wartet die ehemalige Privatsammlung der Brüder Franz Joseph und Hans van der Grinten, mit Exponaten aus dem 19. und 20. Jahrhundert und dem weltweit größten Bestand an

In the Het Nationale Park De Hoge Veluwe the Kroeller-Mueller Museum awaits the visitors with its extensive collection of art work by van Gogh, Seurat, Picasso, Léger, Mondrian and many other classical modern artists. The founder, Helene Kroeller-Mueller, was the art enthusiast daughter of a German industrialist and married the dutchman Kroeller in 1888.

One of the largest sculpture gardens in the world forms part of the museum. Over an area of 25 hectares a large number of sculptures by well-known artists of the 20th century are exhibited.

In the Moyland Castle, the former private collection of the brothers Franz Joseph and Hans van der Grinten has exhibits from the 19th and 20th Century and the world's largest collection of work by

Links/Oben: Skulpturengarten Kröller-Müller-Museum

Left/above: Sculpture garden Kroeller-Mueller-Museum

Arbeiten von Joseph Beuys auf. Ebenfalls hier untergebracht ist das Joseph Beuys Archiv, das auch als internationale Forschungseinrichtung dient.

Xanten gilt als die Römer-, Dom- und Siegfriedstadt am Niederrhein. Besonders sehenswert ist der archäologische Park auf dem Gelände der Römerstadt Colonia Ulpia Traiana mit zahlreichen rekonstruierten Bauten aus der Römerzeit.

In Duisburg ist die beeindruckende Revitalisierung des alten Innenstadthafens zu erleben. Sehenswert, neben vielen anderen Bauwerken, sind die erste bewegliche Hängebrücke der Welt, der „Garten der Erinnerung" des Bildhauers Dani Karavan mit zeitgenössischen Kunstprojekten im Haus Trinks, das

Links: Xanten
Rechts: Hafen Duisburg

Joseph Beuys. Likewise the Joseph Beuys archives, which also serve as an international research facility, is accommodated here.

Xanten has the status of Roman, cathedral and Siegfried town on the Lower Rhine. Particularly well worth seeing is the archaeological park on the site of the Roman city of Colonia Ulpia Traiana with numerous reconstructed buildings from the time of the Romans.

In Duisburg the impressive regeneration of the old city centre port is something to be experienced. In addition to many other structures, well worth seeing is the world's first moveable suspension bridge, the "Garden of Remembrance" by the sculptor Dani Karavan with contemporary art projects in the Trinks House, the Kuep-

Left: Xanten
Right: Harbour Duisburg

Museum Küppersmühle mit Exponaten bedeutender Nachkriegskünstler aus der Sammlung des Unternehmers Hans Grothe, sowie das über die Grenzen hinweg bekannte Museum der Stiftung Wilhelm Lehmbruck: Errichtet zu Ehren des expressionistischen Duisburger Bildhauers Lehmbruck gibt es mit über 300 Skulpturen und Objekten einen umfassenden Eindruck in das Schaffen des international renommierten Künstlers des 20. Jahrhunderts.

Auch Essen ist für Kunstinteressierte eine Reise Wert. Hier erwartet das Deutsche Plakat Museum seine Gäste: eine Sammlung mit über 80.000 Exponaten illustriert die Geschichte des Plakats.

Im Museum Folkwang ist eine umfangreiche Sammlung deutscher und französi-

Links: Lehmbruck Museum
Rechts: Museum Folkwang, Essen

persmuehle Museum with exhibits by prominent post-war artists from the entrepreneur Hans Grothe's collection, and the Wilhelm Lehmbruck Foundation Museum well known beyond the borders of Germany - established in honour of the Duisburg expressionist sculptor Lehmbruck, with over 300 sculptures and objects it gives a comprehensive impression of the internationally renowned 20th century artist's work.

A trip to Essen is for art enthusiasts highly recommendable. The German Poster Museum awaits visitors here: a collection of over 80,000 exhibits illustrates the history of the poster.

In the Folkwang Museum an extensive collection of German and French paintings as well as sculptures from the 19th

Left: Lehmbruck Museum
Right: Museum Folkwang, Essen

scher Malerei sowie Skulpturen aus dem 19. und 20. Jahrhundert zu bewundern, u. a. von Caspar David Friedrich, Corot, Courbet, Monet, Manet, van Gogh, Matisse, Pollock, Rothko und Baselitz.
Auch die Villa Hügel, das ehemalige Wohnhaus der Industriellen-Familie Krupp am Essener Baldeneisee, ist als Gebäude ebenso sehenswert, wie die dort bereits seit 1953 stattfindenden Ausstellungen von internationalem Rang.
Ein besonderes Kleinod ist das Weltkulturerbe Zeche Zollverein. Die einst in Anlehnung an den Bauhausstil errichtete Schachtanlage ist heute ein Industriedenkmal von internationaler Bedeutung. Hier sitzt das Design Zentrum NRW. Eine einmalige Ausstellung zum Industriedesign in den alten Hallen der Kokerei und Führungen zur Bergbaugeschichte bieten den Rahmen für bleibende Eindrücke.

Oben: Villa Hügel, Essen
Rechts: Zeche Zollverein, Essen

and 20th centuries by, amongst others, Caspar David Friedrich, Corot, Courbet, Monet, Manet, van Gogh, Matisse, Pollock, Rothko and Baselitz, are to be admired.
Also the Huegel Villa on Lake Baldeney in Essen, the former residence of the Krupp family, is just as worth seeing for the grandness of its architecture, as it is for the international exhibitions held inside since 1953.
A special gem is the world cultural heritage site Zollverein Coalmine. The pit, once built in the Bauhaus style, is today an industrial monument of international importance. The North-Rhine Westphalia design centre is located here. An unique exhibition of industrial design in the old halls of the coking plant and guided tours of the history of the mining industry – experiences that provide for lasting impressions.

Above: Huegel Villa, Essen
Right: Zeche Zollverein, Essen

Zollverein

German Castles
GAST IM SCHLOSS

SCHLOSSHOTEL KURFÜRSTLICHES AMTSHAUS

Gastgeberinnen/hostesses: Petra & Christa Probst

54550 Daun/Vulkaneifel · Germany
Telefon: +49 (0) 6592-9250 · Fax: +49 (0) 6592-925255
www.daunerburg.de
kurfuerstliches.amtshaus@t-online.de

Das Hotel
Inmitten der Kurstadt Daun, auf dem Basaltgestein eines erloschenen Vulkans, liegt das Kurfürstliche Amtshaus. Die stilvoll eingerichteten Zimmer mit antikem Mobiliar, historischen Betten und wunderschönen Uhren aus den verschiedensten Epochen erwarten die Gäste. In der Ritterbar „Grafenschänke" lässt es sich, wie im Mittelalter, in ritterlicher Atmosphäre tafeln. Das Gourmet-Restaurant „Graf Leopold" bietet kreative Küche auf hohem Niveau.

The hotel
The 'Kurfürstliches Amtshaus' lies in the midst of the spa town of Daun, built on the basalt rock of an extinct volcano. Stylishly furnished rooms with antique furniture, historical beds and beautiful clocks from the most diverse periods await the guests. In the "Grafenschaenke" knight bar you can feast in a knightly atmosphere as in the Middle Ages. The Count Leopold gourmet restaurant offers excellent quality creative cuisine.

Hotel

Restaurant

Angebot/facility

(3) 80 €

(26) 118-155 €

A/S (1) 200 €

(3) 20-90

20 km

120 km

Anfahrt/journey

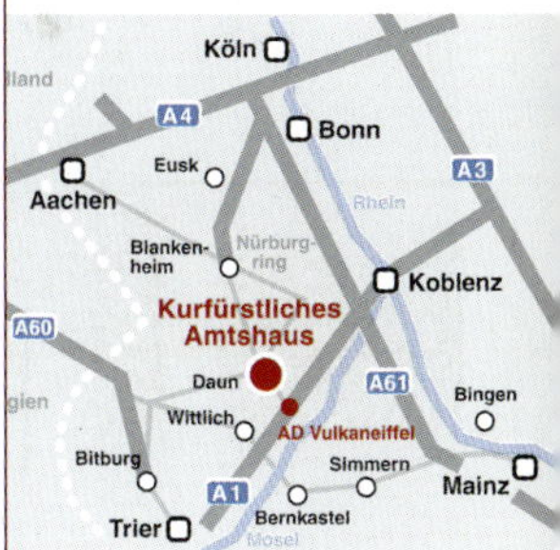

Das Kurfürstliche Amtshaus entstand 1712 zusammen mit einem Jagdschloss, das der Trierer Kurfürst Karl-Joseph, Herzog von Lothringen, während der Renovierung der Burg erbaute. Verschiedene Burgherren, darunter Kelten, Römer, Franzosen und Preußen, haben hier gelebt, doch der berühmteste Bewohner der Dauner Burg war sicher Leopold von und zu Daun, der im Siebenjährigen Krieg den Alten Fritz bei Kolin und Hochkirch besiegte. 1758 wurde er zum Oberbefehlshaber der gesamten österreichischen Streitmacht ernannt. Heute ist das Gourmet-Restaurant „Graf Leopold" nach ihm benannt. An die vulkanreiche Umgebung erinnert das Schwimmbad, eingemeißelt in Lavagestein eines vor Jahrtausenden erloschenen Vulkans, das zusammen mit Sauna, Dampfbad und Solarium Erholung und Entspannung bietet.

The 'Kurfürstliches Amtshaus' was constructed in 1712 together with a hunting lodge, that the Trier Elector Karl Joseph, Duke of Lorraine, built during the renovation of the castle. Various Lords of the castle, among them Celts, Romans, French and Prussians, lived here, but the most famous inhabitant of the Dauner Castle was surely Leopold of and to Daun, who defeated the "Old Fritz" in Kolin and Hochkirch during the Seven Year's War. In 1758 he was appointed the commander in chief of the entire Austrian armed forces. Today the "Count Leopold gourmet restaurant" is reminiscent of him. The swimming pool, engraved in the lava rock of a volcano extinct thousands of years ago, is also evocative of the volcanic-rich surroundings and together with the sauna, steam bath and solarium offers recovery and relaxation.

In der näheren Umgebung:
Daun: Eifel Vulkanmuseum, Wilderlebnispark, Sommerrodelbahn; **Brockscheid (4 km):** Besuch der Glockengießerei; **Dauner Maare (5 km):** Schwimmbad und Bootsverleih; **Mückeln (15 km):** Korbflechtstadt; **Nürburgring (18 km):** Rennstrecke, Rennsportmuseum, Freizeitpark-Erlebniswelt, Fahrsicherheitszentrum; **Meisburg (20 km):** mit Wasserkraft betriebene Schneidemühle; **Maar-Mosel-Radweg:** ab Schloss Start bis Bernkastel/Mosel 55 km oder nach Manderscheid auf dem Lieserpfad.

In the surrounding area:
Daun: The Eifel Volcanic Museum, 'Wilderlebnispark' wild animal park, summer toboggan run; **Brockscheid (2 miles):** Visit to the bell foundry; **Dauner Maare (3 miles):** Swimming pool and boat hire; **Mückeln (9 miles):** wicker work town; **Nuerburgring (11 miles):** Racing course, racing museum, recreational park/discovery world, driving safety centre; **Meisburg (12 miles):** Water powered sawmill; **Maar-Mosel cycle path:** starting from the castle departure point on 34 miles to Bernkastel/Mosel or to Manderschied on the Lieser trail.

ReiseArt Tipp!

Eine in Europa einmalige Sehenswürdigkeit ist der Ort Wallenborn mit seiner vulkanischen Quelle. Der von Kohlendioxid, und nicht wie bei Geysiren sonst üblich durch Hitze, angetriebene Geysir erreicht mit seiner Fontäne eine Höhe bis zu 3 m. Zu den weiteren geologischen Besonderheiten der Region gehört die Lava- und Vulkanbombe bei Strohn, eine 2000 Zentner schwere, 6 m hohe und 4 m breite Basaltkugel.

A unique landmark in Europe is Wallenborn with its volcanic source. The geyser, activated by carbon dioxide rather than heat, as is the case normally with geysers, reaches a height of up to 3 m with its fountain. An additional geological characteristic of the region is the lava and volcanic bomb near Strohn, which is a 2000 hundredweights heavy, 6m high and 4m wide basalt ball.

German Castles
GAST IM SCHLOSS

BURGHOTEL AUF SCHÖNBURG

Gastgeber/host: Fam. Huettl

55430 Oberwesel · Germany
Telefon: +49 (0) 6744-93930 · Fax: +49 (0) 6744-1613
www.hotel-schoenburg.com
huettl@hotel-schoenburg.com

Das Hotel
Hoch oben auf der Schönburg, mit Blick über den Rhein, befindet sich dieses romantische Hotel in einer 1.000-jährigen Burg. Geschichte und zeitgemäßer Komfort gehen hier eine harmonische Verbindung ein. Zauberhafte Zimmer mit Himmelbetten, stilvollen Bädern und liebevollen Details laden den Gast zum genussvollen Verweilen ein. Feinschmeckermenüs werden von Servicegeistern entweder im gemütlichen Restaurant oder auf der Rheinterrasse serviert.

The hotel
This romantic hotel is located high up above in the 1,000 year old Schoenburg Castle with a view over the Rhine. History and modern comfort combine here in harmonious connection. Enchanting rooms with four poster beds, stylish bathrooms and lovingly added details invite the guest to have a highly enjoyable stay. Gourmet menus are offered with waiter service either in the cosy restaurant or on the Rhine terrace.

Hotel 🛎🛎🛎🛎
Restaurant 🍸🍸🍸🍸

Angebot/facility

(2) 85-105 €

(20) 150-210 €

A/S (2) 215 €

(2) 6-43

2 km

90 km

Anfahrt/journey

Erstmalig erwähnt wurde die Burg 1149, wobei jedoch davon auszugehen ist, dass der Bau wesentlich früher entstanden ist. Im 14. Jahrhundert lebten auf der Ganerbenburg etwa 250 Nachkommen aus dem Geschlecht der Schönburger gleichzeitig, da alle Burggrafensöhne erbberechtigt waren. Der letzte Schönburger erwarb als französischer General im 17. Jahrhundert viel Ruhm, bevor die Burg 1689 von den Truppen Ludwigs XIV. niedergebrannt wurde. Ab 1885 restaurierte der Bankier Rhinelander, ein einflussreicher Deutsch-Amerikaner, große Teile der Burg. Seit 1957 besitzt Familie Huettl das Anwesen. Seitdem wurden die Restaurierungen kontinuierlich fortgesetzt und ein Burghotel geschaffen.

The castle was first mentioned in 1149, however it is to be assumed that the building was established a good deal earlier. In the 14th century about 250 descendants from the House of Schoenburg lived in the Ganerben Castle at the same time, since all the sons of the burgrave were entitled to inherit. The last of the Schoenburgs acquired much fame, as a French general in the 17th century, before the castle was burned down in 1689 by the troops of Ludwig XIV. In 1885 the influential German American banker Rhinelander, restored large parts of the castle. Since 1957 the Huettl family has owned the estate. Since then the restorations were continued and a castle hotel was established.

In der näheren Umgebung:
Oberwesel: mittelalterliche Stadt inklusive Wehrtürmen, Stadtmauern; im Kulturhaus wechselnde Kunstausstellungen und Veranstaltungen; **Bacharach (5 km):** mittelalterliches Städtchen; **Loreley (5 km):** sagenumwobener Felsen mit der Geschichte vom schönen Mädchen, das durch seinen betörenden Gesang und seine fesselnde Schönheit die Schiffer in den Tod trieb (Besucherzentrum).

In the surrounding area:
Oberwesel: medieval town with defence towers, town walls; in the cultural centre there are changing art exhibitions and events; **Bacharach (3 miles):** small medieval town; **Loreley (3 miles):** legendary rock with the story of the beautiful girl, who with her enticing singing and her binding beauty led the skippers to their death (Visitor centre).

ReiseArt Tipp!

UNESCO-Weltkulturerbe „Oberer Mittelrhein“: Tour 1: Ab Oberwesel mit dem Schiff nach Assmannshausen. Von dort mit der Sesselbahn zum Jagdschloss Niederwald und zur „Germania“. Mit der Kabinenbahn hinunter nach Rüdesheim. Von dort mit der Rheinfähre nach Bingen. Mit dem Zug zurück nach Oberwesel.
Tour 2: Mit dem Fahrrad auf dem Schiff von Oberwesel nach Boppard. Von dort mit der Hunsrückbahn nach Emmelshausen. Mit dem Fahrrad über den Hunsrück-Radwanderweg zurück nach Oberwesel.

UNESCO world cultural heritage “upper middle Rhine”: Route 1: Starting from Oberwesel by boat to Assmannshausen. From there with the chair lift to the Niederwald Hunting Lodge and to the "Germania". With the cable car down to Ruedesheim. From there with the Rhine ferry to Bingen. And then by train back to Oberwesel.
Route 2: By boat with the bicycle from Oberwesel to Boppard. From there with the Hunsrueck train to Emmelshausen. By bike over the Hunsrueck cycle path back to Oberwesel.

German Castles
GAST IM SCHLOSS

SCHLOSS RHEINFELS

Gastgeber/host: Gerd Ripp

Schlossberg 47 · 56329 St. Goar · Germany
Telefon: +49 (0) 6741-8020 · Fax: +49 (0) 802802
www.schloss-rheinfels.de
info@schloss-rheinfels.de

5.3

Das Hotel
Auf den Rheinhöhen, gegenüber dem legendären Loreleyfelsen liegt das Schlosshotel Rheinfels. Das mehrmals zum besten Tagungshotel Deutschlands ausgezeichnete Haus lädt mit seiner modernen Ausstattung in mittelalterlicher Anlage zum Verweilen ein. Kulinarisch verwöhnt wird der Gast mit Produkten aus der hauseigenen Patisserie und der regionalen, saisonalen Küche im Restaurant „Kanonenzimmer" oder im Sommer auf der Rheinterrasse mit dem wunderbaren Blick auf das Loreleytal.

The hotel
The Rheinfels Castle Hotel lies above the River Rhine, opposite the legendary Loreley Rock. The hotel, which has on several occasions been acknowledged as the best conference hotel in Germany, with its modern furnishings in a medieval building, is an inviting place for guests to stay. The guest is spoilt in the culinary sense with products from the hotel patisserie and the regional, seasonal kitchen in the "Kanonenzimmer" Restaurant or in the summer on the Rhine terrace with the marvellous view of the Loreley Valley.

Hotel
Restaurant

Angebot/facility

(6) 85-140 €

(49) 128-185 €

A/S (4) 155-260 €

(9) 10-150

1,5 km

40 km

Anfahrt/journey

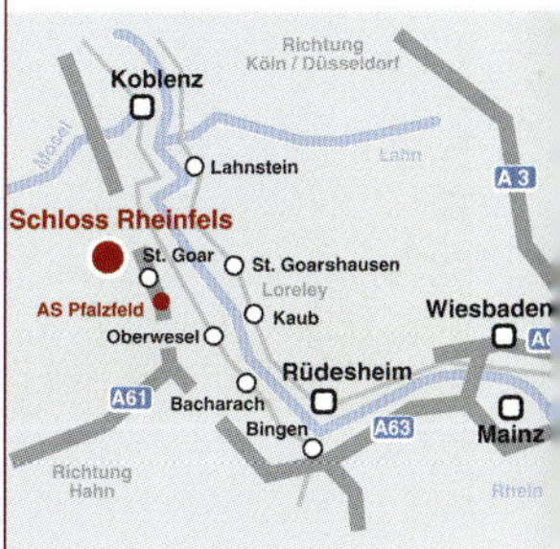

Die 1425 vom Grafen Diether V. von Katzenelnbogen erbaute Burg Rheinfels entwickelte sich im Laufe der Jahrhunderte zur bedeutendsten Festung am Rhein. Anfangs diente die Burg hauptsächlich der Zollsicherung. Im 16. und 17. Jahrhundert wurde sie zur Festung ausgebaut. Heute zeugen die Ruinen von der einstigen Macht dieser mittelalterlichen Burg, die um 1795 größtenteils gesprengt wurde. Diese Kulisse bietet alljährlich den idealen Schauplatz für das Ritterturnier und Theateraufführungen. Seit das Schloss unter der Leitung von Gerd Ripp steht, hat es zahlreiche positive Veränderungen erfahren. So wurde nicht nur Europas größter Gewölbekeller der Öffentlichkeit gastronomisch zugänglich gemacht, sondern auch ein stilvoller, 300 qm großer Wellnessbereich errichtet.

The Rheinfels Castle, built in 1425 by Count Diether V of Katzenbogen, developed over the centuries into the most formidable fortress on the Rhine. At first the castle served mainly as a tax collecting office. In the 16th and 17th Century it was developed into a fortress. Today the ruins stand witness to the former power of this medieval castle, which was blown up to a large extent around 1795. This backdrop offers the ideal setting for the annual knight tournament and theatre performances. Since the castle has been under the direction of Gerd Ripp, it has experienced numerous positive changes. Thus not only Europe's largest vault was made gastronomically accessible to the public, but a more stylish, 300 m^2 spa area was also built.

In der näheren Umgebung:
Burg Rheinfels: wechselnde Ausstellungen in der „Großen Wachstube"; Heimatmuseum; **St. Goar:** Deutsches Puppen- und Bärenmuseum; Wahrschauer- und Lotsenmuseum; Anlegestelle für Ausflugsschifffahrt, z. B. vorbei am Loreleyfelsen, an imposanten Burgen, von Bingen bis Koblenz; **UNESCO-Weltkulturerbe „Oberer Mittelrhein":** Wander- und Fahrradausflüge, z. B. IVV-Rundwanderweg auf insgesamt 120 km mit sieben Themenwegen.

In the surrounding area:
Rheinfels Castle: changing exhibitions in the "Großen Wachstube"; local history museum; **St. Goar:** German Puppet and Bear Museum; River Watchman and Pilot Museum; Landing place for boat trip e.g. past the Loreley Rock, impressive castles, from Bingen to Koblenz; **UNESCO world cultural heritage "upper middle Rhine":** Walking and bicycle trips, e.g. IVV circular walk altogether 120 km with seven themed walks.

ReiseArt Tipp!

Der Natur- und Erlebnispfad zählt zu den besonderen Attraktionen. Die Kombination aus Natur-Lehrpfad und Outdoor-Aktionselementen führt auf einem Kilometer entlang der alten Befestigungsmauern der Burg, mitten durch die Waldlandschaft, vorbei an kleinen Teichen, Lichtungen und einem natürlichen Wasserfall. Ob barfuß über Moos, Kies und Stein, Holzhacken oder abseilen, hier kommen sportlich Ambitionierte, Naturliebhaber und Erholungssuchende gleichermaßen auf ihre Kosten.

A nature and adventure trail is among the special attractions. The combination of nature trail and outdoor action elements leads for a kilometre along old castle fortress walls, through the middle of the forest landscape, past small ponds, clearings and a natural waterfall. Whether barefoot over moss, gravel and stone, wood chip or roping, the sportily ambitious, as well as nature lovers and those looking for relaxation alike come here and get their money's worth.

Auf den Spuren der Romantik an Mosel und Rhein

Die Moseluferstraße führt über 193 km von Trier nach Koblenz durch eine pittoreske Landschaft und zahlreiche romantische Winzerorte, vorbei an imposanten Burgen (Burg Eltz und Burg Cochem). Sehenswert, auch für einen längeren Aufenthalt, ist Alt-Cochem mit seinen Befestigungsanlagen und zahlreichen alten Giebelhäusern. Die „Alte Thorschenke" gehört zu den ältesten und besonders gut erhaltenen Weinlokalen. Trier, im Jahre 16. v. Chr. von Kaiser

On the trail of romance on the Rivers Mosel and Rhine

The Moseluferstrasse (Banks of the River Mosel Road) leads for 120 miles from Trier to Koblenz through a picturesque landscape and numerous romantic winegrowing areas, past impressive castles (Castle Eltz and Castle Cochem). Worth seeing, also for a longer stay, is Old Cochem with its fortification and numerous old gable houses. The "Alte Thorschenke" belongs to the oldest and particularly well preserved wine restaurants.
Trier, established in 16 B.C. by the Emperor Augustus, is considered to be

Links: Porta Nigra: römisches Stadttor aus dem 2. Jahrhundert, Trier
Oben: Matthias Basilika, Trier

Left: Porta Nigra: Latin citygate from the 2nd century, Trier
Above: Basilica Matthias, Trier

Augustus gegründet, gilt als älteste deutsche Stadt. Etwa 100 Jahre später entstand das heute noch in Teilen erhaltene Amphitheater, das ursprünglich 20.000 Zuschauer fassen konnte. Von der römischen Zeit zeugen noch weitere Gebäude, wie die Kaiser-, Barbarathermen, die Thermen am Viehmarkt, die Aula Palatina sowie das römische Stadttor Porta Nigra.

Seit 273 n. Chr. ist Trier Bischofssitz, wovon der Dom, als älteste Bischofskirche Deutschlands ein einducksvolles Zeugnis ablegt. Der Dom gehört heute zum UNESCO-Weltkulturerbe und dokumentiert über 1.650 Jahre Architektur- und Kunstgeschichte.

In Trier steht auch das Geburtshaus von Karl Marx, dem Begründer der politischen Ökonomie. Die Dauerausstellung

the oldest town in Germany. About 100 years later the amphitheatre was built, which could originally accommodate 20,000 spectators and parts of which still remain today. The time of the Romans is still to be witnessed through other buildings, such as the Imperial Baths, the Barbara Baths, Forum Baths at the Cattle Market, the Aula Palatina as well as the Roman fortified town gate, the 'Porta Nigra'.

Since 273 A.D. Trier has been the bishop's see, whose cathedral, as the oldest bishop's church, bears a formidable testament. The cathedral today belongs to UNESCO world cultural heritage and documents over 1,650 years of architectural and artistic history.

The birth house of Karl Marx, the founder of political economy, is also situated in

Oben: Kaiserthermen

Above: Emperor Thermal Springs

im Karl-Marx-Haus vermittelt anhand von Originaldokumenten einen interessanten Eindruck über sein Leben und sein philosophisches Schaffen.
Am Zusammenfluss von Mosel und Rhein liegt Koblenz, eine Stadt mit bedeutsamer Geschichte. Seit der Zeit der Römer

Trier. The permanent exhibition in the Karl Marx House with original documents, provides an interesting insight into his life and philosophical work.
Koblenz is situated at the confluence of the River Moselle and the River Rhine, a city with a meaningful history. Since the

Oben: Romanischer Dom St. Peter und Liebfrauenkirche (13. Jh.), Trier
Unten links: Karl-Marx-Relief an seinem Geburtshaus, Trier
Unten rechts: Steipe mit Marktbrunnen, Trier

Above: Romanic Cathedral St. Peter and Church of Our Lady, Trier
Down left: Relief of Karl Marx at his birthplace
Down right: Steipe with market fountain

hat die Stadt in ihrer exponierten Lage große strategische Bedeutung.
An einer Landzunge, direkt an der Mündung der Mosel in den Rhein, liegt das „Deutsche Eck“ mit einem monumentalen Kaiser-Wilhelm-Denkmal. Unweit davon erinnert das Deutschherrenhaus an den Deutschen Ritterorden, der sich 1216 hier ansiedelte.
Auf der anderen Rheinseite liegt die Festung Ehrenbreitstein, eine von den Trierer Kurfürsten vor rund 1.000 Jahren angelegte Burganlage.
Sehenswert ist auch die Kaiserin-Augusta-Anlage, eine schöne Uferpromenade des Gartenbaukünstlers Peter-Joseph Lenné sowie die Basilika St. Kastor: hier verhandelte Ludwig der Fromme 842 über die Teilung des fränkischen Reichs.
Von Koblenz aus gibt es zwei Möglichkeiten, das romantische Rheintal flussaufwärts zu entdecken. Die linksrheini-

time of the Romans, the city, in its exposed position, has been of great strategic importance.
The “German Corner” with an impressive Emperor Wilhelm monument is situated on a headland lying directly on the delta of the Moselle in the River Rhine. Nearby the German manor house is a reminder of the German Order of Knights, who settled here in 1216.
On the other side of the Rhine lies the Ehrenbreitstein Fortress, a castle commissioned about 1,000 years ago by one of the Trier Electors.
Worth seeing is also the Empress Augusta Gardens, a beautiful riverside promenade by the horticultural artist Peter Joseph Lenné, and the St. Castor Basilica - it was here that Louis the Pious negotiated about the division of the Franconian Empire in 842.
From Koblenz there are two possibilities of discovering the romantic Rhine Valley

Links: Historiensäule, Koblenz
Unten: Blick auf Koblenz und das „Deutsche Eck“

Left: Historic Pillar, Koblenz
Down: View over Koblenz and the German Corner

sche Strecke führt über Boppard, St. Goar, Oberwesel und Bacharach nach Bingen und weiter durch das Nahetal nach Bad Kreuznach. Die rechtsrheinische Strecke verläuft über Lahnstein, an der Loreley vorbei, nach Kaub, Lorch, Assmannshausen, nach Rüdesheim und weiter durch den Rheingau nach Wiesbaden. Die Rheinseite kann unterwegs problemlos gewechselt werden, entlang der Strecke gibt es sechs Auto- und vier Personenfähren.
Erste Station ist das historische Städtchen Boppard, keltischen Ursprungs und mit bis zu 8 m hohen Mauern eines spätrömischen Kastells umgeben. Über St. Goar thront die imposante Burg Rheinfels, einst von den

upstream. The route left of the Rhine leads through Boppard, St.Goar, Oberwesel and Bacharach to Bingen and further along the Nahe Valley to Bad Kreuznach.
The route right of the Rhine continues through Lahnstein, past the Loreley Rocks, to Kaub, Lorch, Assmanshausen to Ruedesheim and further along the Rhine region to Wiesbaden. It is possible along the route to change sides of the Rhine without any problem, as along the way there are six car ferries and 4 foot passenger ferries.
First stop is the historical small town of Boppard, of celtic origin and surrounded by walls of a late Roman fort up to 8 m high.
Enthroned above St.Goar is the impressi-

Oben: Festung Ehrenbreitstein

Above: Fortress Ehrenbreitstein

Grafen von Katzenelnbogen zur Sicherung des Rheinzolls erbaut, beherbergt die riesige Anlage heute ein einladendes Schlosshotel. An den Burgen Katz und Maus vorbei gelangt man zur Loreley, dem Mittelpunkt der Rheinromantik und in vielen Liedern besungen. In Oberwesel, der „Stadt der Türme und des Weins", mit einer auch heute noch beeindruckenden, mittelalterlichen Stadtumwehrung, grüßt schon von weitem die 1.000-jährige Schönburg hoch über der Stadt. Auch sie beherbergt ein romantisches Hotel. „Steinernes Schiff" heißt die alte Zollfestung bei Kaub, die auf einer Insel mitten im Rhein errichtet wurde.

Das idyllische Weinstädtchen Bacharach ist gleich von mehreren Burgen, den

Links: Loreley
Rechts: Alte Zollfestung „Steinernes Schiff"

ve Rheinfels Castle, built by one of the Counts of Katzenelnbogen to protect the Rhine customs post, the colossal construction today accommodates an inviting castle hotel. After having passed the Cat and Mouse Castles, you then arrive at the Loreley Rocks, the centre of romance on the Rhine and mentioned in many songs. In Oberwesel, the "town of towers and wine" with a still impressive, medieval town rampart, the 1,000 year old Schoenburg Castle greets people from afar high above the town. It too accommodates a romantic hotel.

The old customs fortress near Kaub named "Stone Ship" was erected on an island in the middle of the River Rhine.

The idyllic small wine town of Bacharach is

Left: Loreley
Right: Old Custom Fortress „Steinernes Schiff"

Burgen Stahleck, Sooneck, Rheinstein und Reichenstein, umgeben.
Ebenfalls auf einer winzigen Insel mitten im Rhein steht der Mäuseturm, ein Wahrzeichen von Bingen. Auch er wurde ursprünglich als Wacht- und Zollturm gebaut. Sein Name leitet sich somit von dem auch heute so gebräuchlichen Begriff „Maut“ ab, die hier von den Schiffern erhoben wurde.
Sehenswert in Bingen ist auch die Burg Klopp, die teilweise auf Fundamenten der Römerzeit errichtet wurde und die Mündung der Nahe in den Rhein markiert, sowie die Rochuskapelle auf dem gleichnamigen Berg, mit einem von Goethe gestifteten Bild des heiligen Rochus.

Oben: Burg Sooneck

surrounded by several castles – Stahleck, Sooneck, Rheinstein and Reichenstein Castles.
Also standing on a tiny island in the middle of the Rhine is the “Mouse Tower”, one of Bingen's landmarks. It too was built originally as a watch and customs tower. Its name itself refers to the term "toll" still commonly used today, which was collected here from the boat operators. Well worth seeing in Bingen are also Klopp Castle, which was partly established on Roman foundations and which marks the delta of the Nahe in the River Rhine, and the St. Rochus Chapel on the mountain of the same name, with a picture of the holy Rochus donated by Goethe.

Above: Castle Sooneck

Auf der anderen Rheinseite liegen Assmannshausen, die „Heimat des letzten deutschen Rotweins", der allerdings von erstaunlich hoher Qualität ist. Hier steht auch das Niederwalddenkmal, errichtet zum Gedenken an den Sieg über Frankreich und die Gründung des Deutschen Kaiserreichs 1871.
Unterhalb des Denkmals erreicht man in Richtung Wiesbaden den berühmten Weinort Rüdesheim mit dem Rheingau Weinmuseum und der Drosselgasse, einem beliebten Treffpunkt für feuchtfröhliche Weingelage.

Links: Assmannshausen
Rechts: Drosselgasse in Rüdesheim
S. 88: Der „Koblenzer Schengel" Symbolfigur der Stadt

On the other side of the Rhine is Assmannshausen, the "home of the last German red wine", which is indeed of an amazingly high quality, and the Niederwald Memorial, erected in commemoration of the unification of Germany in 1870/71.
Downstream of the Niederwald Memorial heading towards Wiesbaden you reach the famous wine town of Ruedesheim with the Rhineland Wine Museum and Drosselgasse (Thrush Lane), a popular meeting place to spend a merry evening drinking wine.

Left: Assmannshausen
Right: Thrush Alley in Ruedesheim
P. 88: "Schengel" a symbol of Koblenz

German Castles
GAST IM SCHLOSS

HOTEL ALTE THORSCHENKE

Gastgeber/host: Herr/Mr. Dudeck

Brückenstrasse 3 · 56812 Cochem (Mosel) · Germany
Telefon: +49 (0) 2671-7059 · Fax: +49 (0) 2671-4202
www.castle-thorschenke.com
alte-thorschenke@t-online.de

Das Hotel

Die Hotelzimmer der Alten Thorschenke in Cochem sind historisch eingerichtet mit antikem Mobiliar aus der Mosel-Gegend und laden zum Träumen in schönen Himmelbetten ein. Wählen kann man auch zwischen Suiten, denen frühere Herrscher wie Napoleon oder Maria Theresia ihre Namen gegeben haben. Im stilvollen Weinrestaurant bietet eine reichhaltige Speisekarte moselländische Spezialitäten sowie Wild- und Fischgerichte.

The hotel

The rooms of the Alte Thorschenke Hotel in Cochem on the River Mosel are historically furnished with antique furniture from the Mosel area and invite you to dream on beautiful four-poster beds. You can also choose between suites, to which former rulers such as Napoleon or Maria Theresia gave their names. The stylish wine restaurant offers a varied menu of Mosel specialities, game and fish dishes.

Hotel 🛎 🛎 🛎

Restaurant 🍸 🍸 🍸

Angebot/facility

(3) 50-78 €

(30) 86-125 €

A/S (3) 135-155 €

(2) 25-80

0,5 km

40/170 km

Anfahrt/journey

Die heute zu den bekanntesten alten Weinschenken gehörende Alte Thorschenke ist Bestandteil der vom Trierer Kurfürsten Balduin, Graf von Luxemburg, 1332 erbauten Stadtbefestigung und des Endertores. Anfangs als Wohnung des Wallmeisters und als Sammelort der Bürgerwehr genutzt, beherbergte sie später Reisende, die hier einkehrten, um ihre Reise mit der Postkutsche nach Frankfurt und Köln zu beginnen oder zu unterbrechen. Zur Zeit der Romantik war sie bei Malern und Dichtern sehr beliebt und stets eng verbunden mit der Geschichte der Stadt und der Reichsburg. Heute stimmen bereits die geschnitzte alte Baumwendeltreppe und die alten Kaminplatten im Entrée den Gast auf die behagliche und urgemütliche Atmosphäre des historischen Hauses ein.

The Alte Thorschenke, today belonging to the most well-known old wine bars, is an integral part of the town's fortified walls, constructed in 1332 by the Elector of Trier Balduin, Count of Luxembourg, and of the Ender gateway. Initially used as the master of the rampart's residence and as an assembly point for the militia, it later accommodated travellers starting or interrupting their journey by stage coach to Frankfurt and Cologne. In the Romantic period, it was very popular with painters and poets and was always closely connected with the history of the city and the realm castle. Today the carved old tree spiral staircase and the fireplace plates in the entrance hall set the mood for the comfortable and cosy ambiance of the historical house.

In der näheren Umgebung:
Cochem: mittelalterliche Altstadt mit der weltberühmten Reichsburg; **Cochem-Beilstein (ca. 15 km):** Ausflug mit der Moselflotte zum Dornröschen der Mosel; **Eller (ca. 18 km):** Weinproben auf dem hauseigenen Weingut; **Calmont (ca. 20 km):** steilster Weinberg Europas; **Burg Eltz (ca. 30 km):** Burgführung möglich, Besuch der Schatzkammer, Weinprobe und Führung durch das 500 Jahre alte Weingut „Baron von Landenberg".

In the surrounding area:
Beilstein: Boat trip on the River Mosel to the "Sleeping Beauty" of the River Mosel Eltz Castle: Guided tour of the castle possible, visit to the treasury; **Calmont:** Europe's steepest vineyard; **Cochem:** Medieval part of town with the world-famous realm castle; **Eller:** Wine tasting in the hotel's own vineyard, Wine tasting and guided tour through the 500 year old "Baron of Landenberg" vineyard.

ReiseArt Tipp!

Ein Aufenthalt an der Mosel ist eng mit dem Moselriesling verbunden. Verschiedene Winzer der Region präsentieren während der Moselweinwoche im Frühjahr ihre Weine. Das alljährliche Weinfest findet am letzten Wochenende im August statt. Die „Happy Mosel" lädt Radfahrer, Fußgänger und Inlineskater zur Nutzung der für den Autoverkehr gesperrten Straße zwischen Trier und Cochem ein.

A stay on the River Mosel is closely connected with the Mosel Riesling. Different winegrowers of the region present their wine during the Mosel wine week from 25th to 29th May 2005. The annual wine festival takes place on the last weekend in August. At "Happy Mosel" time on 22nd May, cyclists, pedestrians and inline skaters can use the road closed to traffic between Trier and Cochem.

German Castles
GAST IM SCHLOSS

BURGHOTEL SCHNELLENBERG

Gastgeber/hosts: Stephan & Thomas Bilsing

Schnellenberg 1 · 57439 Attendorn · Germany
Telefon: +49 (0) 2722-6940 · Fax: +49 (0) 2722-694169
www.burg-schnellenberg.de
info@burg-schnellenberg.de

Das Hotel
Komfortable, stilvoll eingerichtete Zimmer heißen die Gäste auf Burg Schnellenberg willkommen. Das elegante Restaurant im Gobelinsaal, der rustikale Rittersaal mit Kamin sowie die Bar im Wappenkeller mit der Terrasse im Innenhof und Blick auf Attendorn bieten eine vielseitige Küche und einen gut sortierten Weinkeller. Die wunderschöne Renaissancekapelle aus dem 16. Jahrhundert und ein Standesamt ermöglichen Hochzeiten, Taufen und Festlichkeiten jeder Art.

The hotel
Comfortable, stylishly furnished rooms welcome the guests to Schnellenberg Castle. The elegant restaurant in the Gobelin Hall, the rustic Knights Hall with fireplace, as well as the bar in the coat of arms cellar with the terrace in the inner courtyard and view over Attendorn, all offer a versatile cuisine and a well-assorted wine cellar. The beautiful Renaissance Chapel from the 16th century with the registry office enable weddings, baptisms and festivities of every kind to take place here.

Hotel
Restaurant

Angebot/facility

(3) 85-105 €

(37) 120-165 €

A/S (2) 180-190 €

(8) 80-120

24/25.12., 5 Tage
Neujahr

3 km

49/86 km

Anfahrt/journey

Über den grünen Hügeln des Sauerlands thront die im Jahre 1222 erstmals urkundlich erwähnte Burg Schnellenberg. Die hoch aufragenden Wachtürme, das mächtige steinerne Torgewölbe, die schweren eisenbeschlagenen Türen, die Schatzkammer mit mittelalterlichen Sehenswürdigkeiten lassen noch heute die Vergangenheit erkennen. 1594 ging die Burg mit allem Grundbesitz an Caspar von Fürstenberg über und ist seitdem im Besitz der Familie. Hier findet der Besucher Gastlichkeit mit jahrhundertealter Tradition vor und wird bereits am oberen Torweg mit dem in grauen Sandstein gemeißelten Spruch
„Foris non maneat peregrinus. Ostium meum pateat viatori! Draußen nicht bleibe der Fremdling. Meine Tür öffne sich dem Reisenden!“ empfangen.

The Schnellenberg Castle, mentioned in records for the first time in 1222, reigns over the green hills of the Sauerland region. The past is still to be seen represented today by the high rising watch towers, the powerful stone archways, the heavy iron-fitted doors and the treasure chamber with medieval objects of interest. In 1594 the castle with its whole estate became the property of Caspar of Fuerstenberg and has since then been owned by the family. Here the visitor can find hospitality with centuries old of tradition and is greeted at the upper gateway by the following dictum chiselled in grey sandstone:
"Foris non maneat peregrinus. Ostium meum pateat viatori! Stranger do not stay outside. My door is open to the traveller!"

In der näheren Umgebung:
Attendorn (3 km): Hansestadt mit Rathaus aus dem 14. Jahrhundert, Sauerländer Dom mit mehr als 900 Jahren Geschichte, Südsauerlandmuseum, Atta-Tropfsteinhöhle; **Biggesee (6 km):** Westfalens größte Talsperre, Wassersport, Ausflugsfahrt mit der Weißen Flotte;
Elspe (18 km): Karl-May-Festspiele (www.elspe.de); **Kirchhundem (25 km):** Panoramapark am Rothaarsteig: 80.000 qm großer Freizeitpark.

Around the hotel:
Attendorn (2 miles): Hanseatic town with town hall dating from the 14th century, Sauerland Cathedral with more than 900 years of history, South Sauerland Museum, Atta stalactite cave; **Bigge Lake (4 miles):** Westphalia's largest dam, water sports, trip on the 'Weiße Flotte' boat; **Elspe (11 miles):** Karl May festivals (www.elspe.de); **Kirchhundem (15 miles):** Panorama park at the Rothaarsteig: 800 m^2 recreational park.

ReiseArt Tipp!

„Guet Führ" heißt es jedes Jahr zu Ostern in Attendorn. Am Gründonnerstag, wenn die Orgel und Glocken während des Abendgottesdienstes verstummen, beginnt der Osterbrauch. „Die Stunden werden geblasen", die Kinder ziehen geräuschvoll mit Ratschen um die Kirche, die Ostersemmel wird gesegnet, das obligatorische Osterfeuer wird entzündet. All dies und mehr sorgt für ein schönes und ganz besonderes Osterfest.

"Guet Fuehr" is what is said each year at Easter in Attendorn. On Maundy Thursday, when the organ and bells are silenced during the evening service, the Easter custom begins. A horn is sounded on the hour every hour, the children run around the church with rattles, the Easter bread is blessed, the compulsory Easter fire is lit. All this and more makes for a beautiful and completely special Easter.

Auf den Spuren der Nibelungen

Der Sage nach zogen die Nibelungen von Worms, ihrer zeitweiligen Hauptstadt, über die heutige Nibelungen- oder die Siegfriedstraße zu Hunnenkönig Etzel an die Donau ins gegenwärtige Ungarn. Worms und Würzburg sind die Endpunkte beider Straßen. Die nördliche Nibelungenstraße hat eine Länge von ca. 150 km, die südliche Siegfriedstraße erstreckt sich über ca. 160 km.
Worms ist die älteste Stadt Deutschlands und trotz großer Zerstörungen im 17./18. Jahrhundert sowie im Zweiten Weltkrieg sind einige interessante Sehenswürdigkeiten erhalten.
Ferner können Nibelungen- und Siegfriedstraße auf einer Rundreise erlebt werden. Diese führt durch wunderschö-

On the trail of the Nibelungen

According to the legend, the Nibelungen went from Worms, their temporary capital city, over the present day Nibelungen and Siegfried Road to King Etzel of Hun region on the River Danube in the present day Hungary. Both roads end at Worms and Wuerzburg Castle. The northern Nibelungen Road is approx. 95 miles long, the southern Siegfried Road extends over approx. 100 miles.
Worms is the oldest town in Germany and despite experiencing extensive damage in the 17th and 18th centuries, as well as during the Second World War, some interesting landmarks still remain.
Furthermore Nibelungen and Siegfried Road can be discovered on a round trip. This leads through wonderful varied land-

Links: *Hagendenkmal, Worms*

Left: *Monument of Hagen, Worms*

ne abwechslungsreiche Landschaften, historische Städte, vorbei an sagenumwobenen Burgen und imposanten Bauwerken.

Um den westlichen Teil der beiden Straßen (Worms, Bürstadt, Lorsch, Bensheim) zu erkunden, empfiehlt sich das Parkhotel Herrenhaus als Ausgangspunkt für eine Tagesreise über Lindenfels, Michelstadt, Erbach, Miltenberg und Freudenberg weiter auf der Nibelungenstraße nach Würzburg. Dort lädt das Schlosshotel Steinburg mit seinem atemberaubenden Blick auf die alte Residenzstadt ein. Es lohnt sich hier mindestens zwei Nächte zu verweilen, um ausreichend Zeit zur Erkundung Würzburgs und der am Main aufwärts liegen-

Links: Jüdischer Friedhof, Worms
Rechts: Liebfrauenkirche, Worms

scapes, historical towns, past legendary castles and impressive buildings.

In order to explore the western part of the two roads (Worms, Buerstadt, Lorsch, Bensheim) the Herrenhaus Park Hotel is recommended as a starting point for a day excursion through Lindenfels, Michelstadt, Erbach, Miltenberg and Freudenberg and further along the Nibelungen Road to Wuerzburg Castle. Here particularly inviting is the Steinburg Castle Hotel, with its breathtaking view over the old residential town. It is worthwhile to stay here at least two nights, in order to have sufficient time to explore Wuerzburg Castle and the sloped wine-growing areas along the River Main. The next stage leads through Wertheim,

Left: Jewish cemetery, Worms
Right: Church of Our Lady, Worms

den Weinorte und Winzer zu haben. Die nächste Etappe führt über Wertheim, Tauberbischofsheim und Walldürn nach Amorbach zum alten Klostergut der Benediktinerabtei, dem Landhotel Schafhof. Der Schafhof bietet neben einer exzellenten Küche eine idyllische Wohlfühlatmosphäre, die sich über mehrere Tage genießen lässt, ehe man über die Siegfriedstraße (Hesseneck, Mossautal, Fürth, Heppenheim) wieder zum Ausgangspunkt der Rundreise zurückkehrt.

Sehenswert in Worms sind neben dem Nibelungenmuseum auch der Dom und die älteste Synagoge Deutschlands sowie der älteste Judenfriedhof Europas. Kloster Lorsch mit seiner Königshalle, der

Oben: Abteikirche Amorbach

Tauberbischofsheim and Wallduern to Amorbach at the old monastery property of the Benedictine Abbey, the Schafhof Country Hotel. In addition to the excellent cuisine, the Schafhof offers an idyllic feel-good atmosphere, which can be enjoyed over several days, before making one's way over the Siegfried Road (Hesseneck, Mossau Valley, Fuerth, Heppenheim) back to the starting point of the round trip. Apart from the Nibelungen Museum in Worms, the cathedral as well as the oldest German synagogue and the oldest Jewish cemetery in Europe are also highly recommendable sightseeing stops. Lorsch Monastery with Carolingian gate house, church, tithe barn and monastery wall has since 1991 been a

Above: Abbey Church Amorbach

Kirche, mit Zehntscheune und Klostermauer gehört seit 1991 zum UNESCO-Weltkulturerbe. Im Rathaus befindet sich der mit Wandmalereien geschmückte Nibelungensal und gleich nebenan die Ruine der ehemaligen Reichsabtei. Zu besichtigen ist auch das interessante Tabakmuseum.

Bensheim begrüßt seine Besucher mit zahlreichen renovierten Fachwerkhäusern und alten Adelshöfen. Im Stadtteil Auerbach wartet der Staatspark Fürstenlager, die frühere Sommerresidenz der Landgrafen von Hessen-Darmstadt, auf seine Entdeckung.

Ganz in der Nähe, bei Lindenfels, befindet sich im Lautertal das Felsenmeer, ein alter römischer Steinbruch mit zahlreichen Zeugnissen der damaligen Stein-

UNESCO world cultural heritage site. The Nibelungen Hall with mural paintings can be visited in the town hall as can the ruin of the former imperial abbey situated directly next door. The tobacco museum is also of interest.

Visitors to Bensheim are greeted by numerous renovated half-timbered houses and old aristocratic courtyards and in the Auerbach quarter, the "Fuerstenlager" state park, the former summer residence of the landgraves of Hessen Darmstadt, awaits to be discovered.

Very close by, near Lindenfels in the Lauter Valley, is the Felsenmeer, an old Roman quarry with numerous artistic references to stonemasonry from that period. Lindenfels itself is a small romantic town with winding alleyways, a medieval

Links: Torhalle, Lorsch
Rechts: Rathaus, Michelstadt

Left: Gate Hall, Lorsch
Right: City Hall, Michelstadt

metzkunst. Lindenfels selbst ist ein romantisches Städtchen mit verwinkelten Gassen, einem mittelalterlichem Stadtbild und einer sehenswerten Burgruine.

Die nächste Etappe entlang der Nibelungenstrasse ist Michelstadt, eine ebenfalls gut erhaltene mittelalterliche Stadt mit vielen interessanten Gebäuden und Museen.

Weiter geht es nach Erbach, dem Zentrum der Elfenbeinschnitzerei. Die ehemalige Residenzstadt der Grafen zu Erbach-Erbach besitzt eine sehenswerte Altstadt mit einem imposanten Barockschloss und beherbergt neben dem einmaligen Deutschen Elfenbeinmuseum auch das Schlossmuseum mit den gräflichen Sammlungen.

Die Weiterreise führt über Miltenberg, eine romantische, mittelalterliche Klein-

townscape and a castle ruin well worth visiting.

The next stop along the Nibelungen Road is Michelstadt, a well preserved medieval town with many interesting buildings and museums.

The route continues along to Erbach, the centre of ivory carving. The former residential town of the Counts of Erbach-Erbach has an old part of town well worth seeing, with an impressive baroque castle and, apart from the unique “German Ivory Museum”, it also accommodates the castle museum with the Counts' collection.

The next stage of the journey leads through Miltenberg, a small, romantic, medieval town with panache, to Freudenberg.

The ancient small town in Main is situa-

Oben: Schloss Erbach

Above: Castle Erbach

stadt mit Flair, nach Freudenberg. Das uralte Mainstädtchen liegt in besonders landschaftlich idyllischer Lage. Sehenswert sind die Freudenburg, die Giebelhäuser sowie die Friedhofskapelle mit freigelegten Fresken sowie das Schiffs- und Küfereimuseum.

In Würzburg endet die Nibelungenstraße. Die alte Residenzstadt mit ihren prächtigen Barockhäusern lädt auch zu einem längeren Aufenthalt ein. Die Fürstbischöfliche Residenz gehört zum UNESCO-Weltkulturerbe. Von Würzburg aus geht es über die Siegfriedstraße wieder zurück nach Worms, zum Ausgangspunkt der Rundreise auf den Spuren der Nibelungen.

ted in a particularly idyllic scenic position. Well worth seeing is the Freudenburg Castle, the gable houses as well as the cemetery chapel with exposed frescoes and the ship and cooperage museum.

The Nibelungen Road ends at Wuerzburg. The old residential town with its magnificent baroque houses is the perfect place for longer breaks too. The "Princely Residence" is a UNESCO world cultural heritage site. From Wuerzburg it continues over the Siegfried Road heading back to Worms again, to the starting point of the round trip on the trail of the Nibelungen. First stop is Wertheim, an old Fran-

Oben: Mainblick, Miltenberg

Above: View over the Main, Miltenberg

Erste Station ist Wertheim, ein altfränkisches Kleinod mit malerischer Altstadt, gelegen an der Mündung der Tauber in den Main. Über Tauberbischofsheim mit seiner historischen Altstadt und zahlreichen Sehenswürdigkeiten und Denkmälern (z. B. Renaissance-Torbogen, neugotisches Rathaus, Klosterhof und Klosterkirche) geht es über Walldürn, dem bekannten Wallfahrtsort mit sehenswerter Barockkirche und prächtiger Orgel, vorbei an römischen Ausgrabungen und dem Limeslehrpfad nach Amorbach. Hier steht in einer Abteikirche aus dem 18. Jahrhundert die größte Barockorgel Europas.

conian gem with its quaint older part of town, on the delta of the River Tauber in the Main. Via Tauberbischofsheim with its historical old part of town and numerous places of interest and monuments (e.g. Renaissance archways, neo-Gothic town hall, monastery garden and church) it continues through Wallduern, the well-known place of pilgrimage with baroque church and magnificent organ, Roman excavations and the Limes Nature Trail well worth seeing on to Amorbach. An abbey church from the 18th century with the largest baroque organ in Europe can be found here.

Rechts: Abteikirche, Amorbach
Links: Marktplatz, Heppenheim

Right: Abbey Church, Amorbach
Left: Market place, Heppenheim

German Castles
GAST IM SCHLOSS

SCHLOSSHOTEL ROTHENBUCH

Gastgeber/host: Peter Bernhard Lehnardt

Schloss · 63860 Rothenbuch · Germany
Telefon: +49 (0) 6094-9440 · Fax: +49 (0) 6094-944444
www.schloss-rothenbuch.de
office@schloss-rothenbuch.de

Das Hotel

Das Schlosshotel Rothenbuch im Hochspessart begeistert seine Gäste mit historischem Ambiente. Die Zimmer sind zum größten Teil mit Antiquitäten ausgestattet. Für Allergiker stehen Zimmer mit Parkettboden oder Fliesen zur Verfügung, ebenso gibt es spezielle Zimmer für Gäste mit Hund. Die Küche bietet eine gehobene frische deutsche Küche mit fränkischen Spezialitäten und natürlich Wild aus dem Spessart. Das im orientalischen Stil gestaltete Badehaus erwartet den Gast zum Entspannen.

The hotel

The Rothenbuch Castle Hotel in the Hochspessart region thrills its guests with historical ambience. The rooms are to a large extent furnished with antiques. For those who suffer from allergies, rooms with parquet flooring or tiles are available, equally there are special rooms for guests with a dog. The kitchen offers a refined fresh German cuisine with Franconian specialities and of course game from the Spessart Forest. The oriental styled baths awaits the guests for relaxation.

Hotel 🛎🛎🛎🛎

Restaurant 🍸🍸🍸

Angebot/facility

(10) 62 €

(28) 95-189 €

A/S (5) 95-119 €

(10) 10-250

14 km

70 km

Anfahrt/journey

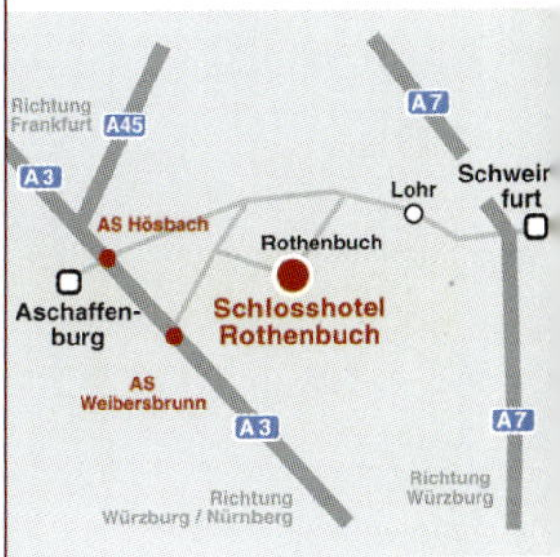

Erstmals erwähnt wird Schloss Rothenbuch in einer Urkunde vom 3. Juli 1318, in der zwischen dem Erzbischof von Mainz und dem Bischof von Würzburg ein Bündnis zur „Abwendung von Untaten ihrer Untertanen“ geschlossen wurde. Erzbischof Daniel Brendel von Homburg ließ 1567 das Schloss in seiner noch heute erhaltenen Form bauen. Dass es sich hierbei um ein ehemaliges Wasserschloss, umgeben von einem forellenreichen See, handelt, lassen die Umfassungsmauern und die beiden Zugangsbrücken erkennen. Für nahezu zweihundert Jahre war das Schloss der zentrale Verwaltungssitz für die gesamte Spessart-Region. Seit 1994 befindet sich das Haus im Eigentum der Familie Lehnardt, die das Schlosshotel seit 1996 als 4-Sterne-Hotel betreibt.

Rothenbuch Castle was first mentioned in a document dating back to 3rd July 1318, in which an alliance for the "prevention of crimes of their subjects" was formed between the Archbishop of Mainz and the Bishop of Wuerzburg. In 1567 Archbishop Daniel Brendel of Homburg had the castle built in the form still preserved today. The surrounding walls and both entrance bridges lay testament to the fact that it was previously a moated castle surrounded by a lake full of trout. For almost two hundred years the castle was the central administrative seat for the entire Spessart region. Since 1994 the property has been owned by the Lehnardt family, which have run the castle as a 4 Star hotel since 1996.

In der näheren Umgebung:
Aschaffenburg (22 km): Schloss Johannisburg mit sehenswerter Gemäldegalerie in der Staatsgalerie, Pompejanum (röm. Wohnhaus), Jüdisches Dokumentationszentrum, Brentano-Brunnen; **Lohr (14 km):** Spessartmuseum mit Schneewittchenspiegel; eine Führung durch das Glasmuseum ist nach Anmeldung möglich; **Schloss Mespelbrunn (14 km):** Drehort des Films „Das Wirtshaus im Spessart" mit Lieselotte Pulver: Spaziergang durch den Park und Führung durch die Räume möglich.

In the surrounding area:
Aschaffenburg (14 miles): Johannisburg Castle with picture gallery in the State Gallery is worth seeing, Pompejanum (a Roman villa), Jewish documentation centre, Brentano Well; **Lohr (9 miles):** Spessart Museum with Snow White Mirror; a guided tour through the Glass Museum is possible after having pre-booked; **Mespelbrunn Castle (9 miles):** Film location of the film „The Spessart Inn" with Lieselotte Pulver: walk through the park and guided tour of the rooms are possible.

ReiseArt Tipp!

Zum genussvollen Entspannen im Schlosshotel Rothenbuch lädt das Gourmet & Wellness Wochenende ein. Während dieses dreitägigen Arrangements können die Gäste erholsame Stunden im Badehaus mit Sauna, Dampfbad, Solarium und Naturtauchbecken verbringen, die Umgebung erkunden und sich mit einem sechs-Gang-Menü kulinarisch verwöhnen lassen.

For beneficial relaxation in the Rothenbuch Castle Hotel the gourmet & spa weekend is on offer. During the three day stay the guests can spend relaxing hours in the bath house with sauna, steam bath, solarium and natural water pool, explore the surroundings and be treated to a six course menu.

German Castles
GAST IM SCHLOSS

DER SCHAFHOF AMORBACH

Gastgeber/hosts: Vera & Herbert Ullrich

Schafhof 1 · 63916 Amorbach · Germany
Telefon: +49 (0) 9373-97330 · Fax: +49 (0) 9373-4120
www.schafhof.de
rezeption@schafhof.de

Das Hotel

Inmitten des traumhaft schönen Naturparks Bayerischer Odenwald liegt der Schafhof Amorbach, ein ehemaliges Klostergut. Die komfortablen Zimmer im luxuriös-ländlichen Stil offenbaren eine Symbiose aus Tradition und zeitgemäßer Modernität. Das Gourmet-Restaurant Abt- und Schäferstube bietet moderne, französische Küche auf Sterneniveau, das Restaurant Benediktinerstube ländlich mediterrane Spezialitäten.

The hotel

The Schafhof of Amorbach, a former monastery, lies in the midst of the fantastically beautiful Bavarian Odenwald Nature Park. The comfortable rooms in the luxurious rustic style reveal a traditional and modern symbiosis. The Abbott and Shepherd Parlour gourmet restaurant offers modern, first class French cuisine, whilst the Benedictine Parlour restaurant offers rural Mediterranean specialities.

Hotel

Restaurant

Angebot/facility

105 €

(16) 130-170 €

A/S (8) 210-275 €

(7) 12-120

Schäferst. Mo./Di.

Benedikt. Mi./Do.

3 km

85 km

Anfahrt/journey

Das ehemalige Klostergut Amorshof der Benediktinerabtei Amorbach, der heutige Schafhof, wurde 1446 erstmals urkundlich erwähnt. 1721 und 1974 liebevoll renoviert, übernachtet man heute in den alten Gemächern der Mönche oder den kleinen gemütlichen Zimmern des ehemaligen Klosterspeichers. Wundersam zurückversetzt in eine andere Zeit machen Tradition und Ausstrahlung den Schafhof zu einem Ort für Individualisten und Liebhaber ausgefallener Szenerie. Ein idealer Platz fernab der Großstadthektik, wo man in Ruhe arbeiten, tagen und sich erholen kann. Für entspannende, wohlige Momente sorgen nicht nur die erlesenen Produkte und Anwendungen des Vital & Beauty Refugiums, sondern auch die zahlreichen Sportangebote.

The former Amorshof Monastery of the Amorbach Benedictine Abbey, which became today's 'Schafhof', was mentioned for the first time in records in 1446. Lovingly restored in 1721 and 1974, today overnight stays in the old living quarters of the monks or the small cosy rooms of the former loft of the monastery are possible. Wondrously set back in time, tradition and charisma establish the 'Schafhof' as a retreat for individualists and lovers of unusual scenery. An ideal place, far away from the hecticness of the large city, where you can work in peace, hold meetings and recuperate. Not only do the exquisite products and exercises of the 'Vital & Beauty' retreat provide for relaxing, pleasant moments, so do the numerous sporting activities.

In der näheren Umgebung:
Amorbach (ca. 5km): Besichtigung der Schnapsbrennerei Bauer; **Miltenberg (ca. 14 km):** Weinprobe auf dem Weingut, Ausflugsschifffahrt auf dem Main; **Buchen-Eberstadt (ca. 29 km):** Besuch der Eberstadter Tropfsteinhöhle in Buchen-Eberstadt; **Aschaffenburg (ca. 45 km):** Automuseum mit der größten Sportwagensammlung der Welt; **Glashofen-Neusaß (ca. 20 km):** Golf-Schnupperkurs bei der Golfakademie Ergül Altinova; **Miltenberg, Walldürn (ca. 20 km), Michelstadt (ca. 23 km):** Spaziergang in historischen Städtchen.

In the surrounding area:
Amorbach (approx 3 miles): Visit to the Bauer distillery; **Miltenberg (approx 9 miles):** Wine tasting on the vineyard, boat excursion on the River Main; **Buchen-Eberstadt (approx 18 miles):** Visit to the Eberstadt stalactite cave in Buchen-Eberstadt; **Aschaffenburg (approx 28 miles):** Automobile Museum with the world's largest sports car collection; **Glashofen-Neusaß (approx 12 miles):** Golf trial training course at the Erguel Altinova Golf Academy; **Miltenberg, Walldürn (approx 12 miles), Michelstadt (approx 14 miles):** Walking in small, historical towns.

ReiseArt Tipp!

Der Schafhof Amorbach bietet ganzjährig besondere Aktivitäten an, die Sie an der Rezeption erfragen sollten, z. B. Bogenschießen in der Feierscheune oder im Freien, geführte Wanderungen, in den Wintermonaten auch mit Fackeln, Empfang mit Fruchtbowle an den Teichen, im Winter wärmende Lagerfeuer mit Punsch, Besichtigung der Abteikirche in Amorbach mit anschließendem Orgelkonzert.

The Schafhof of Amorbach offers all year round special activities, which you should inquire about at reception, e.g. archery in the leisure activity barn or in the open air, organised walks, also with torches during the winter months, reception with punch at the ponds, warming campfire with mulled wine in the winter, guided tour of the abbey church in Amorbach followed by an organ concert.

Auf den Spuren des Jugendstils

Der Jugendstil entstand etwa 1880 als damals neue Kunstrichtung, mit der die Künstler ein von der Kunst durchdrungenes Leben propagierten, ein Leben, in dem all die den Menschen umgebenden Dinge des täglichen Lebens künstlerisch miteinander in Einklang gebracht werden sollen.
In Ablehnung gegenüber dem damals üblichen Historismus überwogen im Jugendstil der Natur entlehnte Ornamente, abstrahierte Linien und später geometrische Verzierungen. Eines der Zentren des deutschen Jugendstils war Darmstadt. Hier entstand 1899 im

On the trail of art nouveau

Art nouveau developed around 1880 as a new art trend at that time, through which the artists publicised a life penetrated by art. A life, in which the things surrounding humans in daily life were to be artistically reconciled with one another.
In rejection of the traditional historism prevailing in art nouveau of nature at the time, ornaments and abstract lines and later geometrical ornaments were used. One of the centres of German art nouveau was Darmstadt. It was here in 1899 that the Hessian Grand Duke Ernst Ludwig commissioned a living

Links: Mathildenhöhe, Darmstadt
Oben: Hochzeitsturm, Darmstadt

Left: Mathildenhöhe, Darmstadt
Above: Wedding Tower, Darmstadt

Auftrag des hessischen Großherzogs Ernst Ludwig eine Wohn- und Arbeitswelt der dem Jugendstil verpflichteten Kunst: die auch heute noch beeindruckende Künstlerkolonie Mathildenhöhe.
Dazu gehörten u. a. die Architekten Josef Maria Olbrich, Peter Behrens und Hans Christiansen. Ihre Bauten und Inneneinrichtungen, die 1901 zum ersten Mal der Öffentlichkeit präsentiert wurden, begründeten den sog. Darmstädter Stil.

and working sphere developed solely for art nouveau inspired work, named the artists' colony 'Mathildenhoehe', which is still just as impressive today.
Those that formed part of the colony were, amongst others, the architects Josef Maria Olbrich, Peter Behrens and Hans Christiansen. The buildings and interior decoration, which were presented to the public for the first time in 1901, established the so-called Darmstaedt style.

Links oben: Mathildenhöhe Portal Ernst-Ludwig-Haus, Darmstadt
Rechts oben: Hochzeitsturm, Darmstadt
Rechts: Hochzeitsturm Mosaik, Mathildenhöhe

Above left: Mathildenhöhe Portal Ernst-Ludwig-House, Darmstadt
Above right: Wedding Tower, Darmstadt
Right: Wedding Tower mosaic, Mathildenhöhe

ERNST LUDWIG
ELEONORE

HOTEL JAGDSCHLOSS KRANICHSTEIN

Gastgeber/host: Konsul Bernd O. Ludwig

Kranichsteiner Straße 261 · 64289 Darmstadt · Germany
Telefon: +49 (0) 6151-97790 · Fax: +49 (0) 6151-977920
www.hotel-jagdschloss-kranichstein.de
service@hotel-jagdschloss-kranichstein.de

Das Hotel

Das Hotel Jagdschloss Kranichstein ist Bestandteil der 1992 komplett renovierten Schlossanlage und bietet seinen Gästen neben dem schlosseigenen Forst auch eine Kapelle zum Heiraten. Im Restaurant Landgraf Ludwig VIII. werden Speisen aus der deutschen Feinschmeckerküche und eine große Vielfalt an Weinen in stilvoller Atmosphäre serviert. Regionale Weine und Gerichte lassen sich gemütlich in der Jagdschloss-Schänke im Kavaliersbau mit einer herrlichen Gartenterrasse genießen.

The hotel

The Kranichstein Hunting Lodge Hotel forms an integral part of the 1992 completely renovated annex of the lodge and apart from the lodge's own forest, it also offers its guests a chapel for getting married. In the Count Ludwig VIII restaurant meals from the German gourmet kitchen and a large variety of wines are served in a stylish atmosphere. Regional wines and dishes can be comfortably enjoyed in the hunting lodge bar in a knightly style with a wonderful garden terrace.

Hotel

Restaurant

Angebot/facility

150-180 €

(11) 170-200 €

A/S (4) 190-280 €

(7) bis 250

Rest

So. Abend/Mo.

6 km

25 km

Anfahrt/journey

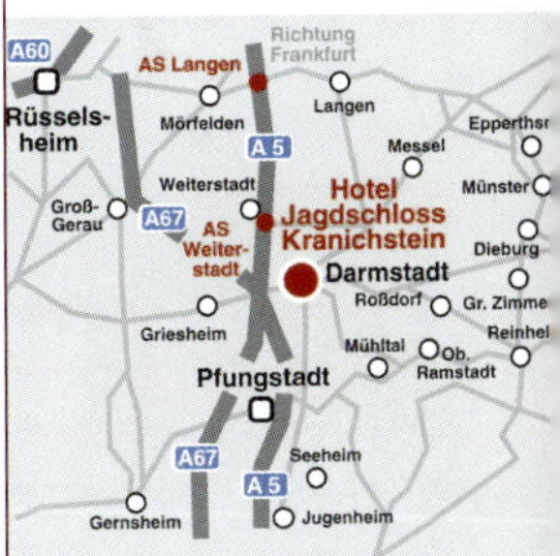

Das Jagdschloss Kranichstein wurde erstmalig 1399 unter „Kranich-Rotth" erwähnt. Zwischen 1578 und 1580 entstanden das zu den wenigen noch erhaltenen Renaissance-Jagdschlössern gehörende Schloss sowie die Schlosskapelle. In der Tradition der unter Landgraf Ernst Ludwig 1708 eingeführten Parforcejagd wurde 1918 unter Großherzog Ernst Ludwig ein Jagdmuseum eröffnet, das noch heute mit seiner einmaligen Sammlung zu besichtigen ist. Das Schlosshotel mit elf Doppelzimmern und vier Suiten hält für das Erkunden des schlosseigenen Forstes in jedem Zimmer einen Spazierstock und, falls es doch mal regnen sollte, auch einen Regenschirm bereit.

The Kranichstein Hunting Lodge was mentioned in records for the first time in the year 1399 under the rule of "Kranich Rotth". The lodge, belonging to the few still preserved Renaissance hunting lodges, as well as the lodge's chapel, were built between 1578 to 1580. Due to the tradition of hunting on horseback introduced under the rule of Count Ernst Ludwig in 1708, a hunting museum was opened in 1918 during the rule of the Grand Duke Ernst Ludwig, which with its unique collection can still be visited today. The lodge hotel with 11 double rooms and 4 suites has ready in each room a walking cane to explore the lodge's own forest and, just in case it should rain, also an umbrella.

In der näheren Umgebung:
Grube Messel (2 km): UNESCO-Weltkulturerbe mit 10.000 Funden zur Entwicklungsgeschichte der Erde; **Darmstadt:** Innenstadt (6 km), Jugendstilensemble Mathildenhöhe, die nach Entwürfen von Friedensreich Hundertwasser errichtete Waldspirale (2 km), die Großherzoglich-Hessische Porzellansammlung im Prinz-Georgs-Palais, Führungen durch das Weltraumoperationszentrum für Satellitenkontrolle (ESOC); **Frankfurt (25 km):** Architektur-, Postmuseum, Museum für moderne Kunst, Schirn Kunsthalle.

In the surrounding area:
Grube Messel (1 mile): UNESCO world cultural heritage with 10,000 finds to do with the history of the development of the earth; **Darmstadt:** City centre (4 miles), Mathildenhoehe (Mathilda's hill) set of art nouveau houses, Friedensreich Hundertwasser 'Waldspirale' spiral house (1 mile), Hessian Grand Duke porcelain collection in Prince George's Palace, guided tours through the space operation centre for satellite control (ESOC); **Frankfurt (15 miles):** Architecture and Post Office Museum, Museum for Modern Art, Schirn Arts Centre.

ReiseArt Tipp!

Das Hotel Jagdschloss Kranichstein lädt regelmäßig zum Dinner-Krimi ein. Eingebettet in ein köstliches Dinner werden die Gäste, die z. B. auf Schloss Coolroy in Schottland die Verlobung der Tochter des Hauses feiern, Augenzeuge eines Verbrechens, das mit der Unterstützung von Scotland Yard gemeinsam gelöst wird. Passend dazu können die Gäste das Arrangement Dinner-Krimi mit zahlreichen Besonderheiten buchen.

Kranichstein Hunting Lodge Hotel regularly invites its guests to a murder mystery dinner. Whilst enjoying a delicious dinner, the guests, who are for example in Castle Coolroy in Scotland celebrating the engagement of the daughter of the residence, become eye witnesses to a crime, that with the assistance of Scotland Yard they must solve together. Keeping to this theme, the guests can ask to have numerous special features incorporated into the murder mystery dinner.

German Castles
GAST IM SCHLOSS

PARKHOTEL HERRENHAUS

Gastgeber/hosts: Adolf & Thilo Patzelt

Staatspark Fürstenlager · 64625 Bensheim-Auerbach · Germany
Telefon: +49 (0) 6251-70900 · Fax: +49 (0) 6251-789689
www.parkhotel-herrenhaus.de
info@parkhotel-herrenhaus.de

Das Hotel
Seit nunmehr 35 Jahren betreibt Familie Patzelt im fürstlichen Herrenhaus ein Hotel mit Feinschmeckerrestaurant und Café. Die Zimmer und Suiten sind mit Biedermeiermöbeln, tibetanischen Teppichen auf Parkettböden und modernen Bädern ausgestattet, antik und modern zugleich. Mitten im Park gelegen eröffnen die Sonnenterrasse sowie das Restaurant den Gästen einen herrlichen Blick auf die Herrenwiese.

The hotel
For 35 years now the family Patzelt have run a hotel with gourmet restaurant and café in the princely manor house. The rooms and suites are furnished, antique as well as modern, with Biedermeier furniture, Tibetan carpets on the parquet floor and modern baths. The sun terrace as well as the restaurant open out in the middle of the park and show the guests a wonderful view of the Herrenwiese.

Hotel
Restaurant

Angebot/facility

(1) 70-90 €

(4) 110-130 €

A/S (4) 150-170 €

(7) 2-150

5 km

50 km

Anfahrt/journey

Die ehemalige Sommerresidenz der Großherzöge von Hessen-Darmstadt und bei Rhein liegt idyllisch in einem Seitental der Hessischen Bergstraße. Im Jahre 1790 als einer der ersten Englischen Gärten auf dem Kontinent von dem berühmten Gartenarchitekten Skell geplant, gilt die Anlage heute als eine der schönsten in Hessen. Der 40 ha große Park mit über 50 exotischen Bäumen und Sträuchern, dem ältesten Mammutbaum Europas, Perückensträuchern und Magnolien verführt zu ausgiebigen Spaziergängen. Von den Teehäuschen, Tempelchen und der russischen Kapelle, die früher die Herrenwiese umgaben, sind nur noch die Voliere und die Hermitage erhalten. Das Hotel wurde 1988 komplett renoviert und im Biedermeierstil eingerichtet.

It was the former summer residence of the Grand Dukes of Hessen-Darmstadt and lies idyllically on the river Rhine in a side valley of the Hessian Mountain Road (hessische Bergstraße). Designed by the famous garden architect Skell in 1790 as one of the first English gardens on the continent, the annex is regarded today as one of the most beautiful in Hessen. The 40 hectare park with over 50 exotic trees and bushes, Europe's oldest mammoth tree, wig bushes and Magnolias entice you on long walks. From the little tee houses, temples and the Russian Chapel, which formerly surrounded the Herrenwiese, only the aviary and the hermitage are preserved. The hotel was completely renovated in 1988 and furnished in the Biedermeier style.

In der näheren Umgebung:
Kloster Lorsch (7 km): Museumszentrum; **Worms (20 km):** Dom, Nibelungenmuseum (zur Sage der Nibelungen Themenspezial Seite 99); **Speyer (40 km):** Historisches Museum der Pfalz, Kulturhof Flachsgasse mit Galerien, Kunstverein, Geburtshaus des Malers Anselm Feuerbach, Fastnachtsmuseum, Technik Museum, Sea Life Aquarium.

In the surrounding area:
Lorsch monastery (4 miles): Museum centre; **Worms (12 miles):** Cathedral, Nibelungen Museum (special themed part about the legend of the Nibelungen) **Speyer (25 miles):** Historical Pfalz Museum, cultural courtyard Flachsgasse with galleries, Art Association, birth house of the painter Anselm Feuerbach, Shrovetide Museum, Technology Museum, Sealife Aquarium.

ReiseArt Tipp!

Insbesondere Weinliebhaber kommen bei einer Tour entlang der Hessischen Bergstraße auf ihre Kosten. Der Ausflug beginnt in Alsbach und führt dann nach Zwingenberg, einem Kleinod mittelalterlicher Fachwerkromantik. In Auerbach lohnt ein Besuch des Schlosses. Weiter geht es nach Bensheim, der größten Stadt der Bergstraße, nach Heppenheim, durch den Odenwald nach Groß- und Klein-Umstadt und über Roßdorf zurück nach Auerbach.

In particular wine lovers get their money's worth with a tour along the Hessian Mountain Road. The trip begins in Alsbach and then leads on to Zwingenberg, a treasure of medieval timber-framed romance. In Auerbach it is worth going to see the castle. It continues on to Bensheim, the largest town of the Mountain Road, Heppenheim, through the Oden Forest to Groß-Umstadt and Klein-Umstadt, and over Rossdorf back to Auerbach.

KLOSTER HORNBACH

Gastgeberin/hostess: Christiane Lösch

Im Klosterbezirk · 66500 Hornbach · Germany
Telefon: +49 (0) 6338-910100 · Fax: +49 (0) 6338-9101099
www.kloster-hornbach.de
hotel@kloster-hornbach.de

Das Hotel

Entspannen können die Gäste in Zimmern mit den unterschiedlichsten Einrichtungsstilen: afrikanisch-asiatischer, aus den Klöstern des Mittelmeerraums stammender mediterraner Stil sowie „Pure Style“, ausgehend von der Glaubensgemeinschaft der Shaker. Die Klosterschänke mit Biergarten bietet regionale Küche, das Restaurant ProVence leichte, mediterrane, kräuterreiche Küche. In der ehemaligen Abtskapelle der Mönche steht ein Standesamt für Trauungen zur Verfügung.

The hotel

The guests are able to relax in rooms furnished in the most varied styles: Afro-Asian, Mediterranean based on the Mediterranean monasteries, as well as “Pure Style” originating from the Shaker religious community. The monastery bar with beer garden offers regional cuisine and the ProVence Restaurant light, Mediterranean cuisine rich in herbs. In the monks´ former Abbots Chapel a registry office is available for weddings.

Hotel 🛎 🛎 🛎 🛎

Restaurant 🍸 🍸 🍸 🍸

Angebot/facility

(3) 97 €

(28) 149 €

A/S (3) 190 €

(8) 150 P.

Mo. Rest.

8 km

30 km

Anfahrt/journey

Das heutige Kloster Hornbach wurde 742 vom Heiligen Pirminius als Benediktinerkloster gegründet. Die sanfte Hügellandschaft der südwestlichen Pfalz entsprach dem Ideal der Mönche für einen Ort der Besinnlichkeit und inneren Einkehr. Das Kloster erfuhr in den folgenden Jahrhunderten eine bewegte Geschichte: von der Blüte einer klösterlichen Wirkungsstätte bis hin zum fast völligen Verfall. Nach mehrjähriger Restauration und Renovierung konnte im Mai 2000 die einstige Klosterruine als Hotel eröffnet werden. Im Museum Historama sowie im Kräutergarten des Urvaters der Botaniker Hieronymus Bock, der als Lehrer und Prediger in Hornbach im 16. Jahrhundert gelebt hat, kann man die Spuren der Vergangenheit entdecken.

The present day Hornbach Monastery was established in 742 by St. Pirminius as a Benedictine monastery. The gentle hill landscape of the southwest Palatinate corresponded with the monks´ ideal place of sanctuary for self-reflection. In the centuries to follow the monastery experienced a moving history: from the blossoming of a small monastery to its nearly complete dereliction. After several years of restoration and renovation, the former monastery ruin was ready to be opened as a hotel in May 2000. Traces of the past can be discovered in the Historama Museum as well as in the herb garden of the founding Father of Botany, Hieronymus Bock, who lived in Hornbach in the 16th century as a teacher and preacher.

In der näheren Umgebung:
Bitche (15 km): Citadelle aus dem 17. Jahrhundert mit ehemaliger Festungsanlage, Garten des Friedens; **Fischbach (30 km):** Biosphärenhaus mit Baumwipfelpfad; **Gersheim (12 km):** römische Ausgrabungen; **Pirmasens (25 km):** Schuhmuseum im Alten Rathaus; **Rodalben (30 km):** Bärenhöhle in größter natürlicher Felsenhöhle der Pfalz; **Zweibrücken (8 km):** Wildrosengarten mit mehr als 3.000 Sorten; **Shoppingideen:** Outlets in Zweibrücken, Pirmasens, Rodalben, Mettlach.

In the surrounding area:
Bitche (9 miles): Citadel from the 17th century with former fortification, Garden of the Peace **Fischbach (19 miles):** Biosphere House with treetop path; **Gersheim (7 miles):** Roman excavations; **Pirmasens (15 miles):** Shoe museum in the old town hall; **Rodalben (19 miles):** Bear cave in the largest natural rock cave in the Palatine; **Zweibrücken (5 miles):** Wild rose garden with more than 3,000 species **Shopping ideas:** Outlets in Zweibruecken, Pirmasens, Rodalben, Mettlach.

ReiseArt Tipp!

Das frühere Klosterleben erkunden kann man bei einem vom Kloster Hornbach ausgehenden, persönlich geführten Klosterspaziergang durch den historischen Teil der Stadt Hornbach. Radtouren mit Picknickkörben, die das Hotel gepackt anbietet, können mit den hoteleigenen Trekking-Bikes durch den Pfälzer Wald, ins nahe Frankreich oder entlang des Mühlenradwegs unternommen werden.

Discover the earlier monastery life on a guided walk through the historical part of the town of Hornbach starting from the Hornbach Monastery. Bicycle rides with pakked picnic baskets, which can be ordered from the hotel, can take place with the hotel's own trekking bikes through the Palatinate Forest, near to the French border or along the mill cycle path.

Auf den Spuren der Pilger und Mönche

Der Dom zu Speyer ist der größte erhaltene romanische Kirchenbau (Länge 134 m, Höhe 34 m) und wird von der UNESCO als bedeutendes historisches und architektonisches Kulturerbe betrachtet. Die Krypta unter dem Ostteil der Kirche ist die größte des Abendlandes.
Der Kaiserdom ist außerdem Ausgangspunkt des Pfälzer Jakobsweges, der über eine nördliche und eine südliche Route durch unberührte Natur und interessante Orte bis zum Kloster Hornbach führt, nach dessen Gründer, dem heiligen Pirminius, die Region Pirminiusland genannt wird.

On the trail of the pilgrims and the monks

The cathedral at Speyer is the largest preserved Roman building of churches (length 134 m, height 34 m) and is regarded by UNESCO as an important historical and architectural cultural heritage site. The crypt under the eastern wing of the church is the largest of the occident.
The imperial cathedral is also the starting point of the Palatinate Jacob's Path, which leads along a northern and a southern path through unspoiled nature and interesting places up to the Hornbach Monastery. The 'Pirminiusland' region is named after its founder, St.Pirminius.
In the Hornbach Historama Museum the history of the monastery and the region

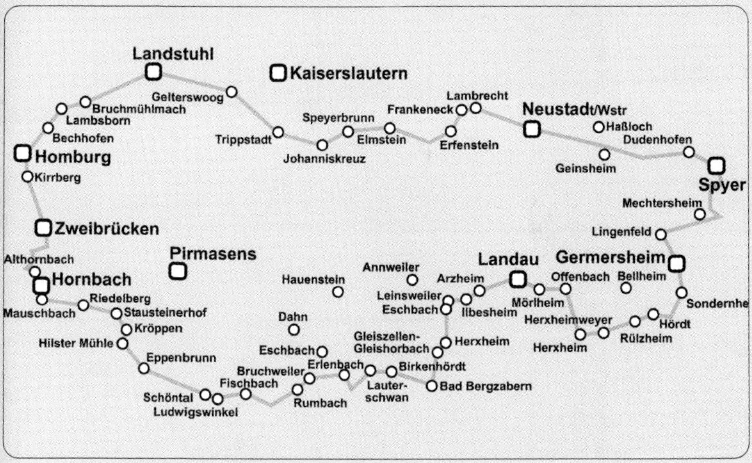

Links: Pilger Dom, Speyer

Links: Pilgrim's Cathedral, Speyer

Im Hornbach-Historama wird die Geschichte des Klosters und der Region auf sehr anschauliche, multimediale Weise entdeck- und erlebbar.

Auf sieben Hügeln wurde die deutsche Schuhmetropole Pirmasens errichtet. Auch sie verdankt ihren Namen dem heiligen Pirminius, dem Begründer des nahe gelegenen Klosters Hornbach. Weite Teile des Pfälzer Jakobsweges säumen pittoreske Winzerdörfer, mächtige Burgruinen und herrliche Ausblicke auf die bezaubernde Landschaft.

Die den Pfälzer Jakobsweg zwischen der Dom- und Kaiserstadt Speyer und dem Kloster Hornbach umgebende Schönheit der Natur lässt sich auch mit

can be discovered and experienced through very animated forms of multimedia.

The German shoe manufacturing metropolis of Pirmasens was built on seven hills. It too owes its name to St. Pirminius, the founder of the nearby Hornbach Monastery. Along the Jacob's Path in Palatinate, picturesque winegrowing villages, impressive castle ruins are to be found and wonderful views of the charming landscape to be enjoyed.

The beauty of nature surrounding the Jacob's Path in Palatinate between the cathedral and imperial city of Speyer and the Hornbach Monastery can also be experienced by car.

Links: Burgruine Elmstein auf der Nordroute
Rechts: Mammutbäume im Pfälzerwald auf der Südroute

Left: Castle ruin on the northern route
Right: Redwoods in the Palatinate forest on the southern route

dem Auto erleben. Wählen kann man dafür zwischen der ca. 125 km langen Nord- und der ca. 132 km langen Südroute.
Die Südroute führt von Speyer über Germersheim, Rülzheim, Herxheim, Landau (schöne Altstadt), Bad Bergzabern (Heilquelle), Birkenhördt, Lauterschwan, Erlenbach, Rumbach, Fischbach, Schöntal, Eppenbrunn, Kröppen und Riedelberg nach Hornbach.
Die Nordroute beginnt ebenfalls in Speyer, und führt über Neustadt, Johanniskreuz, Breitenau, Queidersheim, Landstuhl, Hauptstuhl, Bechhofen, Rosenkopf, Käshofen, Kirrberg, Zweibrücken, Rimschweiler, und Althornbach nach Hornbach.

It is possible to choose from the approx. 78 mile long northern route and the approx. 82 mile long southern route.
The southern route leads from Speyer via Germersheim, Ruelzheim, Herxheim, Landau (beautiful old part of town), Bad Bergzabern (mineral spring), Birkenhoerdt, Lauterschwan, Erlenbach, Rumbach, Fischbach, Schoental, Eppenbrunn, Kroeppen and Riedelberg to Hornbach.
The northern route also begins in Speyer, and leads via Neustadt, Johanniskreuz, Breitenau, Queidersheim, Landstuhl, Hauptstuhl, Bechhofen, Rosenkopf, Kaeshofen, Kirrberg, Zweibruecken, Rimschweiler and Althornbach to Hornbach.

Oben: Kräutergarten im Kloster Hornbach

Above: Herbal garden in Hornbach monastery

German Castles
GAST IM SCHLOSS

HOTEL-RESTAURANT BURG HORNBERG

Gastgeber/host: Freiherr Markus von Gemmingen Hornberg

74865 Neckarzimmern · Germany
Telefon: +49 (0) 6261-92460 · Fax: +49 (0) 6261-924644
www.burg-hotel-hornberg.de
info@burg-hotel-hornberg.de

Das Hotel

Hoch oben über dem Ort Neckarzimmern, zwischen Heidelberg und Heilbronn, thront die imposante Burg Hornberg. Die stilvoll eingerichteten Gästezimmer des Burghotels bieten modernen Komfort hinter historischen Mauern. Von der Café-Aussichtsterrasse und dem Panorama-Restaurant aus offenbart sich ein einzigartiger Blick über das romantische Neckartal. Die Aussicht genießend, können sich die Gäste mit regionalen und internationalen Gerichten verwöhnen lassen.

The hotel

The impressive Castle Hornberg is enthroned high above the village of Neckarzimmern, between Heidelberg and Heilbronn. The stylishly furnished guest rooms of the castle hotel offer modern comfort behind historical walls. From the vantage point of the terrace café or the panoramic restaurant a unique view over the romantic Neckar Valley is revealed. Whilst enjoying the view, the guests can let themselves be spoiled with regional and international dishes.

Hotel 🛎 🛎 🛎 🛎

Restaurant 🍸 🍸 🍸 🍸

Angebot/facility

(3) 78 €€

(19) 100-145 €€

A/S (2) 145-155 €€

(5) 10-130

1/4 km

80 km

Anfahrt/journey

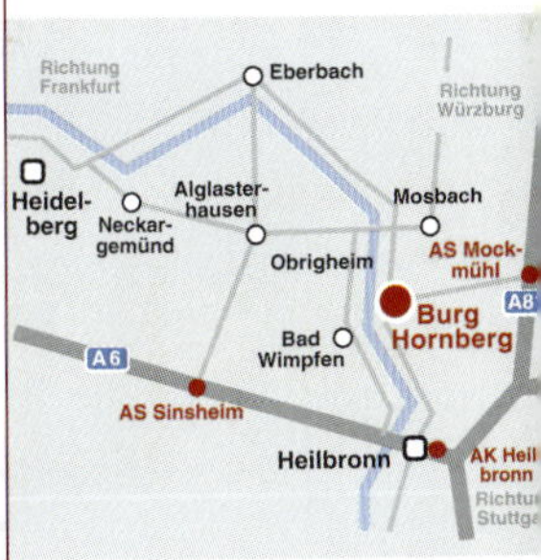

Burg Hornberg gilt als die größte und älteste Burg im Neckartal. Sie wurde im Jahre 1184 erstmals urkundlich erwähnt. Überall kann man teils verborgene Zeugnisse der wechselvollen Burggeschichte entdecken. Nachdem die Burg bereits mehreren Burgherren zu Eigen war, unter anderem den Bischöfen von Speyer, kaufte Götz von Berlichingen die Burg im Jahre 1517. Sie war 45 Jahre lang sein ständiger Wohnsitz, bis er im hohen Alter von 82 Jahren verstarb. Sein Enkel verkaufte die Burg 1612 an die Freiherren von Gemmingen, in deren Familienbesitz sie sich in der nunmehr 12. Generation befindet. 1953 wurde mit dem Ausbau eines Teils der alten Burganlage begonnen und das Hotel-Restaurant Burg Hornberg entstand.

Castle Hornberg is considered the largest and oldest castle in the Neckar Valley. It was mentioned for the first time in documents dating from the year 1184. Partly hidden references to eventful castle history are to be discovered throughout the castle. After having been owned by several lords, amongst others the Bishops of Speyer, Goetz of Berlichingen bought Castle Hornberg in the year 1517. For 45 years it was his permanent residence, until he passed away at the grand old age of 82. His grandson sold the castle in 1612 to the Barons of Gemmingen, whose twelfth generation still own it today. In 1953 the development of part of the old castle annex was started, and the Hotel & Restaurant Castle Hornberg was established.

In der näheren Umgebung:
Mosbach (ca. 7 km): Fachwerkstadt; **Bad Friedrichshall (ca. 15 km):** Besichtigung des Salzbergwerks; **Heilbronn (ca. 25 km):** Rathaus von 1417 mit Renaissance-Einflüssen, Kilianskirche, Deutschhof mit Deutschordensmünster, Götzen- und Bollwerksturm als Relikte der alten Stadtbefestigung, Renaissance-Wasserschloss im Stadtteil Kirchhausen; **Michelstadt (ca. 40 km):** Rathaus im gotischen Fachwerkstil von 1484; **Heidelberg (ca. 55 km):** Heidelberger Schloss und historische Altstadt.

In the surrounding area:
Mosbach (approx 4 miles): City of timber-framing; **Bad Friedrichshall (approx 9 miles):** Visit to the salt mine; **Heilbronn(approx 15 miles):** Town hall of 1417 with Renaissance influences, Kilian's Church, the Deutschhof complex with the Minster of the Teutonic Order, Goetz and Bulwark Tower as part of the relic of the town's fortification, Renaissance moated castle in the Kirchhausen district.; **Michelstadt (approx 25 miles):** Town hall in the gothic framework style of 1484; **Heidelberg (approx 34 miles):** Heidelberg Castle and historical old part of town.

ReiseArt Tipp!

Ohne eine ausführliche Burgbesichtigung sollte man einen Aufenthalt auf der Burg Hornberg nicht beenden. Besonders sehenswert ist zudem die Stauferstadt Bad Wimpfen mit den auch heute noch imposanten Überresten der alten Kaiserpfalz. Der „Wimpfener Götterhimmel“, eine Statuettengruppe, vermittelt einen Eindruck der früheren Verehrung römischer Gottheiten.

A stay at Castle Hornberg would not be complete without having had an extensive guided tour of the castle. Particularly worthwhile to see and visit is also the Staufer town of Bad Wimpfen, where the impressive remains of the old imperial palace can still be seen today. The "Wimpfener Götterhimmel", a group of statues, create the impression of earlier worship of Roman divinities.

Auf den Spuren der Staufer

Da das mittelalterliche Deutsche Reich noch keine Hauptstadt hatte, verteilten sich die „Regierungssitze" - Pfalzen genannt - über das ganze Land. Die Pfalz war ein Ort, in dem höfische Lebensformen gepflegt, Recht gesprochen und von wo aus die dazugehörenden Dörfer und Gebiete verwaltet wurden.
Bad Wimpfen, die größte Kaiserpfalz nördlich der Alpen, ist noch heute eine Attraktion. In idyllischer Lage über dem Neckartal gelegen, mit einer imposanten weithin sichtbaren mittelalterlichen Kulisse und engen Gässchen präsentiert sich die kleine Stadt mit großer Ausstrahlung.
Die interessante Geschichte erlebt man am besten bei einer Stadtführung mit der „Stauferdame".
Vom weithin sichtbaren Blauen Turm bietet sich ein herlicher Blick auf den Necker und die Umgebung.

Links: Blauer Turm, Bad Wimpfen
Oben: Bad Wimpfen

On the trail of the House of Staufer

As the medieval German Reich did not yet have a capital city, the "seats of the government" – called the Palatinates – were distributed throughout the whole country. The Palatinate was a place, in which courtly ways of life were upheld, from where the law and the corresponding villages and areas were administered. Bad Wimpfen, the largest Palatinate north of the Alps, is these days still an attraction. Situated in idyllic surroundings over the Neckar Valley, with an impressive medieval setting and narrow alleyways that can be seen from a great distance above, the small town is bursting with charisma. The best way to discover the interesting history is on a guided tour of the town with a lady in Staufer period dress. The largeley visible Blue Tower invites to wonderful views over the Neckar and the environment.

Left: Blue Tower, Bad Wimpfen
Above: Bad Wimpfen

German Castles
GAST IM SCHLOSS

HOTEL EISENHUT

Gastgeber/host: Jochem F. Eylardi

Herrngasse 3-5/7 · 91541 Rothenburg ob der Tauber · Germany
Telefon: +49 (0) 9861-7050 · Fax: +49 (0) 9861-70545
www.eisenhut.com
hotel@eisenhut.com

Das Hotel

Der Hotelkomplex erstreckt sich über vier, im Inneren mit einander verbundene, ehemalige Patrizierhäuser und bietet seinen Gästen vom romantischen Candle-Light Dinner bis zum mediterranen Flair auf der wunderschönen Gartenterrasse eine aparte Kombination aus Vergangenheit und Moderne. Die Ausstattung der Zimmer besteht durchweg aus Stilmöbeln, angefangen bei den italienischen Tapeten, über die englischen Teppiche bis hin zu den exklusiven Gobelinstoffen.

The hotel

The hotel complex extends over four former patrician houses, all internally linked to each other, and offers its guests a distinctive combination of past and present from romantic candle-lit dinners to Mediterranean panache on the beautiful garden terrace. The rooms are stylishly furnished throughout, from the Italian wallpaper, to the English carpets and the exclusive Gobelin tapestries.

Hotel

Restaurant

Angebot/facility

(14) 106-149 €€

(63) 144-209 €€

A/S 290-340 €€

(9) 80-200

Jan./Feb.

1 km

90 km

Anfahrt/journey

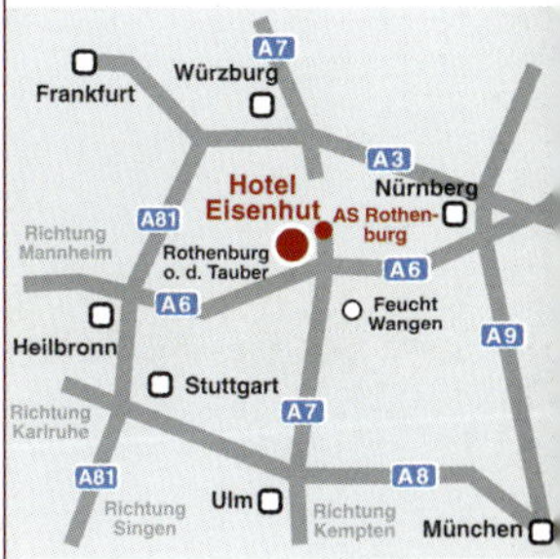

Das Traditionshotel ist seit seiner Gründung im 19. Jahrhundert in Familienbesitz. Auch der heutige Eigentümer Dr. Hans J. Pirner führt im Sinne seiner Vorfahren das Hotel hinter historischen Mauern fort. Im Jahre 1876 eröffnete sein Urgroßvater Georg Andreas Eisenhut in einem der reichen Patrizierhäuser der alten Freien Reichsstadt Rothenburg eine Weinstube, aus der im Laufe der Zeit das heutige Hotel-Ensemble in den vier ehemaligen historischen Bauten im Herzen Rothenburgs entstand. Die gediegene Eleganz der Räume bietet den passenden Rahmen für private Festlichkeiten. Der ausgedehnte Tagungskomplex mit vier Räumen und einer modernen Tagungstechnik ist Garant dafür, dass Seminare oder Besprechungen reibungslos ablaufen.

The traditional hotel is since its establishment in the 19th century under family ownership. The present owner, Dr. Hans J. Pirner, also continues to run the hotel behind historical walls in the same way as his ancestors. In the year 1876 his great-grandfather, Georg Andreas Eisenhut, opened a wine bar in one of the rich patrician houses of the old free imperial town of Rothenburg, which over the course of time has been developed into today's hotel ensemble in the four former historical buildings in the heart of Rothenburg. The pure elegance of the rooms provides suitable surroundings for private festivities. The extended conference complex with four rooms and modern conference technology guarantees that meetings or conferences run smoothly.

In der näheren Umgebung:
Rothenburg ob der Tauber: Stadtbummel durch die verwinkelten Gassen der Stadt der mittelalterlichen Türme, Historiengewölbe im Rathaus, St. Jakobs Kirche, Burggarten, Kriminal-, Puppen- und Spielzeugmuseum, Deutsches Weihnachtsmuseum (bei Käthe Wohlfahrt); **Romantische Straße:** gerne organisiert das Hotel für seine Gäste Ausflüge entlang der Romantischen Straße, z. B. nach Würzburg oder Dinkelsbühl.

In the surrounding area:
Rothenburg ob der Tauber: Stroll through the winding alleyways of the medieval tower town, historical vaults in the town hall, St. Jacob's Church, castle garden, criminal, puppet and toy museum, German Christmas Museum (at the 'Käthe Wohlfahrt' shop); **Romantische Straße (Romantic Road):** the hotel gladly organises trips for its guests along the Romantic Road, e.g. to Wuerzburg or Dinkelsbuehl.

ReiseArt Tipp!

Lassen Sie sich in die Vergangenheit zurückversetzen bei einem Rundgang durch die Stadt mit dem Rothenburger Nachtwächter. In mittelalterlicher Tracht führt er die Gäste zu den bedeutendsten historischen Stellen Rothenburgs.
Eine andere Möglichkeit bietet das Wanderarrangement des Hotels, das täglich frischen Proviant und eine Wanderkarte für die Erkundung der Nebentäler des romantischen Taubertals bereithält.

Let yourself be carried back in time by a tour through the city with the Rothenburger night watchman. In medieval costume he leads the guests to the most important historical places in Rothenburg. Also on offer is the possibility of walking trips organised by the hotel, which include packed lunch and a walking map for exploring the side valleys of the romantic Tauber Valley.

German Castles
GAST IM SCHLOSS

SCHLOSSHOTEL STEINBURG

Gastgeber/host: Lothar Bezold

Auf dem Steinberg · 97080 Würzburg · Germany
Telefon: +49 (0) 931-97020 · Fax: +49 (0) 931-97121
www.steinburg.com
hotel@steinburg.com

Hotel 🛎🛎🛎🛎

Restaurant 🍸🍸🍸🍸

Das Hotel

Innenstadtnah, inmitten der berühmten Weinlage „Würzburger Stein" liegt Schloss Steinburg. Die 52 individuellen Zimmer und historischen Räume sind von elegant bis „franko-mediterran" gestaltet. Hier eröffnet sich ein atemberaubender Panoramablick auf die Residenzstadt, den man von vielen Hotelzimmern sowie von der Sonnenterrasse aus genießen kann. Verwöhnt wird man von der kreativen und prämierten Genussküche von Jena Kirchwitz (Mitglied der „Jungen Wilden").

Angebot/facility

(10) 80-105 €€

(42) 130-155 €€

(6) 50-110

3 km

110 km

The hotel

Steinburg Castle is situated near to the city centre, in the midst of the famous "Wuerzburger Stein" vineyard. The 52 individual bedrooms and historical rooms are designed in elegant to "Franco-Mediterranean" styles. A breath-taking panoramic view over the residential city opens up here, to be enjoyed from many hotel rooms as well as from the sun terrace. You will be spoiled by the creative and award winning indulgent cuisine of Jena Kirchwitz (a member of the "Jungen Wilden").

Anfahrt/journey

Die Ursprünge von Schloss Steinburg gehen zurück auf eine hohenlohische Adelsburg aus dem 13. Jahrhundert – „Castrum in Lapide“ –, ein Gegenstück zur Festung Marienberg. Nach dem diese Burg jedoch zerstört wurde, geriet sie in Vergessenheit. Erst 1897/1898 erbaute Peter Schneider auf dem Würzburger Stein ein romantisches Schloss im Tudorstil. Anfang des 20. Jahrhunderts ging es in den Besitz des Kommerzienrates und Weingroßhändlers G. Meuschel über, der hier 1917 als königlich-bayerischer Hoflieferant mit dem König eine Silvanerrebe pflanzte. Seit 1937 befindet sich das Hotel im Besitz der Familie Bezold, die im Laufe der Jahre das Haus zu einem einzigartigen Hotel ausgebaut hat.

The origins of Steinburg Castle go back to a Hohenlohe aristocratic castle from the 13th century - "Castrum in Lapide" - a counterpart to the Marienberg fortress. After the castle was destroyed however, it was forgotten about. It was not until 1897/1898 that Peter Schneider built a romantic castle in the Tudor style on the Wuerzburger Stein. At the beginning of the 20th century the property came into the hands of the councillor of commerce and wine wholesale dealer G. Meuschel, who, as a Bavarian purveyor to the royal court, planted a silvaner vine here with the king in 1917. Since 1937 the hotel has been owned by the Bezold family, who over the years have continuously renovated and extended the property. Today Steinburg Castle is run by the third generation Lothar Bezold.

In der näheren Umgebung:
Würzburg: Die Fürstbischöfliche Residenz, erbaut 1720 - 1744 von Balthasar Neumann, gehört zum UNESCO-Weltkulturerbe und gilt als das Hauptwerk des süddeutschen Barock; die Altstadt kann man mit einem Nachtwächter erkunden; sehenswert sind Dom, Marienkapelle, Neumünster, Alte Mainbrücke und die Festung Marienberg; **Spessart:** In der Umgebung Würzburgs liegt der Spessart, ein liebliches Mittelgebirge mit malerischen Flusstälern und schönen Wanderrouten und lohnenden Ausflugszielen.

In the surrounding area:
Wuerzburg: Princely Episcopal palace, built between 1720 - 1744 by Balthasar Neumann, belongs to UNESCO world cultural heritage and is considered as the greatest work of the south German baroque period; the old part of the town, which can also be explored with the night watchman, cathedral, Marien Chapel, new cathedral, old Main bridge, Marienberg fortress; **Spessart:** This low mountain range with picturesque river valleys, numerous footpaths and excursion spots lies in close proximity to Wuerzburg.

ReiseArt Tipp!

In Würzburg, dem Zentrum des fränkischen Weinlandes, lässt sich die Welt des Weines am besten bei einer Führung durch die drei historischen Weinkeller der Stadt erkunden: „Der staatliche Hofkeller“, das „Juliusspital“ und das „Bürgerspital zum Heiligen Geist“ gehören zu den schönsten Weinlokalen Deutschlands. Besonders beeindruckend sind die weitläufigen Gewölbe und Kellergänge des Staatlichen Hofkellers.

In Wuerzburg, the heart of Franconian wine country, there are many opportunities on offer to try the different wines. The best way to experience the wine culture is on a guided tour of the three historical wine cellars: “Der staatliche Hofkeller”, “Juliusspital” and "Buergerspital to the Holy Spirit". The extensive bars and cellar passageways of the ‘Staatliche Hofkeller’ are amongst the largest and most traditional in Germany.

German Castles
GAST IM SCHLOSS

HOTEL-RESTAURANT SCHLOSS LANDSBERG

Gastgeber/host: Uwe Klein

Landsberger Straße 150 · 98617 Meiningen · Germany
Telefon: +49 (0) 3693-44090 · Fax: +49 (0) 3693-440944
www.castle-landsberg.com
castle-landsberg@t-online.de

Hotel 🛎 🛎 🛎 🛎
Restaurant 🍸 🍸 🍸 🍸

Das Hotel
Keine reizvolleren Orte als den Rittersaal oder die urige Burgschänke könnte man sich zum erlesenen Speisen oder ritterlichen Mahle erträumen. Aus den aufwendig gestalteten Gemächern des Schlosses haben geschickte Hände ebenso stilvolle wie bequeme Turmzimmer und Himmelbettsuiten entstehen lassen. Den Aussichtsturm von Schloss Landsberg kann man über eine Spindeltreppe emporsteigen. An sonnigen Tagen laden die weitläufige Terrasse oder der Biergarten ein.

The hotel
Whether in the Knights Hall or cosy Castle Bar, you could not dream of a more delightful place to enjoy choice dishes or knightly meals. From the elaborately designed castle apartments, skilled hands have developed stylish as well as comfortable tower rooms and four-poster bed suites. On sunny days you can satisfy your appetite on the extensive terrace or in the beer garden or climb the spiral staircase of the observation tower.

Angebot/facility

95-130 €€

(13) 120-150 €€

A/S (7) 190-220 €€

(4) 8-80

3 km

50 km

Anfahrt/journey

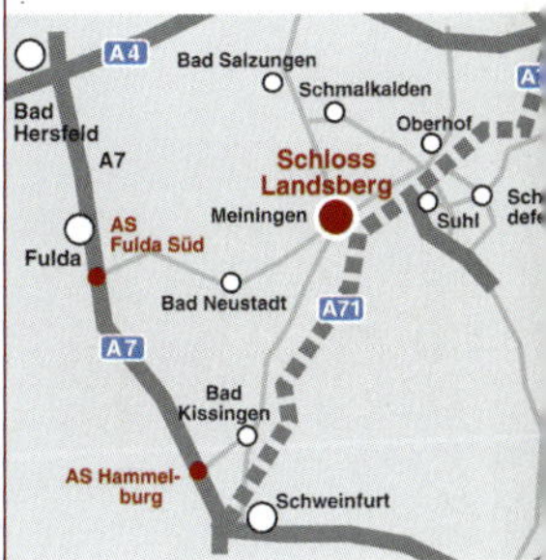

Im Jahre 1836 erwarb Seine Hoheit, Herzog Bernhard II. zu Sachsen-Meiningen, den Hof Landsberg und beschloss auf dem Ruinenhügel, vor den Toren der Theaterstadt, die Wiederaufrichtung eines Schlosses. Seine Schwester, die Königin Adelheid besuchend, hatte er sich in England für die Schlösser der Windsors begeistert und ließ sich in Anlehnung daran von Hofbaurat Doebner zwischen 1836-1844 sein Märchenschloss errichten. Vom romantischen Candle light Dinner in trauter Zweisamkeit bis zur Traumhochzeit in großem Stil; in der wild-romantischen Kulisse der Burg erleben die Gäste in dem erst 2003 komplett sanierten und renovierten Hotel unvergessliche Tage.

Once upon a time... and still today! In the year 1836 Duke Bernhard II. of Saxony Meiningen acquired his sovereignty of the Landsberg court and decided on the 'Ruinenhügel' hill, in front of the gates of the theatre town, to re-erect a castle. Whilst visiting his sister, Queen Adelheid, in England he was inspired by the Windsor castles and did not rest until he had his fairy tale castle built by the chief court architect Doebner between 1836-1844. From the romantic candle-lit dinner in intimate togetherness to the grand dream wedding; in the wild-romantic setting of the castle you will surely spend unforgettable days.

In der näheren Umgebung:
Oberhof (30 km): Luftkurort mit Bob- und Rodelbahn, Sprungschanze, Biathlon-Arena, Rennsteiggarten und Therme; **Erfurt (60 km):** Landeshauptstadt mir histor. Altstadt, Dom, Oper, Zoo, Messe und Gartenausstellung; **Eisenach (60 km):** Lutherstadt mit der berühmten Wartburg, Geburtsstätte von J. S. Bach, Beginn des Rennsteigwanderweges; **Weimar (75 km):** Goethe- und Schillerstadt, Nationaltheater, Bauhausuniversität, Gedenkstätte Buchenwald.

In the surrounding area:
Oberhof (19 miles): Climatic spa resort with bobsleigh and toboggan run, ski jump, biathlon arena, Rennsteig garden and hot springs; **Erfurt (37 miles):** State capital with historical old part of town, cathedral, opera, zoo, fair and horticultural centre; **Eisenach (37 miles):** Luther town with the famous 'Wartburg' castle, birth place of J. S. Bach, start of the Rennsteig footpath; **Weimar (47 miles):** Goethe and Schiller town, national theatre, Bauhaus University, Buchenwald memorial.

ReiseArt Tipp!

Wie wäre es mit einem „schillernden" Kulturwochenende? Harmonisch eingefügt in die Ausläufer von Rennsteig und Rhön finden Sie in Meiningen Theater, Natur und Romantik pur. Und versäumen Sie es nicht, die romantische Freilichtbühne zu besuchen und die original Thüringer Klöße zu probieren, die der Überlieferung nach im Meininger „Schlundhaus" erfunden wurden.

What would you say to a dazzling Schiller culture weekend? Harmoniously located at the foothills of Rennsteig and Rhoen, Meiningen offers theatres, pure nature & romance. And do not miss trying the original Thuringian Kloesse, which according to the tradition was first created in the Meiningen "Schlundhaus", or a visit to the romantic open air stage!

Auf den Spuren Friedrich Schillers

Schillers 200. Todestag 2005 und sein 250. Geburtstag 2009 sind Anlass genug, sich auf seinen Spuren durch Deutschland zu bewegen. Am Beginn seines Lebens und unserer Reise liegt Marbach am Neckar, die Reise endet in Weimar, wo Schiller starb und begraben wurde.
Die ausgewählten Orte dieser Route folgen den Lebensstationen des Dichters

auf doppelte Weise: Zum einen sind sie wichtige Stationen seines künstlerischen Schaffens, zum anderen Orte, die seine Persönlichkeit und seine Sicht auf die Welt entscheidend veränderten.
Am Anfang steht der Sohn eines Militärarztes, der gezwungen wird, sich der Disziplin des Herzogs zu unterwerfen,

Links: Schillerdenkmal, Marbach
Oben links: Schillers Geburtshaus, Marbach
Oben rechts: Schillers Wohnhaus, Weimar

On the trail of Friedrich Schiller

The year 2005 marks two hundred years since the death of Schiller and 2009 his 250th birthday, which are reasons enough to follow his path through Germany. Marbach on the River Neckar is the setting at the beginning of his life and our journey, and Weimar is the end destination, where Schiller died and was buried.
The chosen places on the itinerary follow

the poet's journey through life in two ways: on the one hand they are important places regarding his artistic work, and on the other hand, the places are where his personality and his view of the world decisively changed.
At the beginning, he is the son of an army surgeon, who is forced to submit to

Left: Schiller monument, Marbach
Above left: Schiller's birthplace, Marbach
Above right: Schiller's residential house, Weimar

um selbst zum Militärarzt ausgebildet zu werden. Er fühlt sich jedoch zum Dichter berufen, was der Herzog ablehnt und damit Schillers Freiheitsdrang entfacht. Er desertiert und flieht nach Thüringen, wo er die Bedingungen vorfindet, die ihm die Umsetzung seiner Vorstellungen ermöglichen.

Am Ende steht Schiller als Dichter der Freiheit, einer Freiheit des Einzelnen, die es vor absolutistischer Willkür zu bewahren gilt.

Die Reise beginnt in Marbach, dem Geburtsort Schillers. Hier steht sein

the Duke's discipline in order that he himself be trained as an army surgeon. He however feels destined to be a poet, which the Duke rejects, consequently sparking Schiller's desire for freedom. He deserts the army and flees to Thuringia, where he finds the conditions, that allow him to realise his visions.

In the end Schiller becomes a libertarian poet, who stands for liberty of the individual in need of protection from absolutist arbitrariness.

The journey begins in Marbach, Schiller's birthplace. His birth house and

Links: Schillers Geburtshaus, Marbach
Rechts: Schillerhaus, Ludwigsburg

Left: Schiller's birthplace, Marbach
Right: Schiller's house, Ludwigsburg

Geburtshaus und das Schiller Nationalmuseum mit dem deutschen Literaturarchiv. Seine ersten Theateraufführungen erlebte Schiller in Ludwigsburg, im Barockschloss mit Opernhaus, 1766 das größte Theater in Europa. Nach seiner Flucht nach Thüringen wohnte Schiller als Dr. Ritter in Bauerbach in dem Haus, in dem heute das Schillermuseum untergebracht ist. In der Nähe erinnert die Begegnungsstätte Friedrich Schiller mit der Gaststätte „Zum braunen Ross“ an den

the Schiller National Museum with the German literature archive are to be found here. In 1766 Schiller experienced his first theatre performances in Ludwigsburg, in the baroque castle with opera house, the largest theatre in Europe at the time. After his escape to Thuringia Schiller lived in Bauerbach under the alias of Dr. Ritter, in the house which today accommodates the Schiller Museum. Nearby the 'Friedrich Schiller' meeting place with the "Zum braunen Ross" ("To the Brown Steed") Restaurant

Links: Schillers Unterkunft in Bauerbach
Rechts: Auf dem Weg nach Meinigen überquerte Schiller hier die Werra

Left: Schiller's accommodation in Bauerbach
Right: Travelling to Meiningen Schiller crossed the Werra here

Dichter, sowie das „Naturtheater Friedrich Schiller".

In Meiningen, unweit von Bauerbach entfernt laden das Literaturmuseum Baumbachhaus, das Theatermuseum „Zauberwelt der Kulisse", das Meininger Theater und das Schloss Elisabethenburg ein. Empfohlen sei der Schillerwanderweg von Meiningen nach Bauerbach, auf dem es sich hervorragend auf den Spuren des großen Dichters wandeln lässt.

are reminders of the poet, as is the "Friedrich Schiller Open Air Theatre".

In Meiningen, situated not far away from Bauerbach, you are invited to discover the Baumbachhaus Literature Museum, the "Glamorous world of the stage" Theatrical Museum, the Meiningen Theatre and the Elisabethenburg Castle. The Schiller Footpath from Meiningen to Bauerbach is recommended as a perfect place to walk the path of the great poet.

Oben: Schloss Heidecksburg

Above: Castle Heidecksburg

In Rudolstadt traf Schiller zum ersten Mal in der sehenswerten Heidecksburg die Schwestern von Lengefeld und erhielt in der Glockengießerei (leider heute nur von außen zu besichtigen) die Anregungen zu seinem „Lied von der Glocke“.
Im Leipziger Schillerhaus in Gohlis schrieb Schiller seine Ode an die Freude und im Schillergarten in Dresden (unterhalb des heutigen „Blauen Wunders“) fand er in der Wirtstochter Johanne

It was in the picturesque Heidecksburg Castle in Rudolstadt that Schiller met the Lengefeld sisters for the first time and in the bell foundry (today unfortunately only to be viewed from the outside) came by the stimuli for "The Song of the Bell".
In the Leipzig Schiller House in Gohlis Schiller wrote his 'Ode to Joy' and in the Schiller Garden in Dresden (downstream from the "Blue Miracle" Bridge) he met the landlord's daughter, Johanne Justine

Links: Hier schrieb Schiller seine Ode an die Freude
Rechts: Weinberg Dresden-Loschwitz: Sommersitz von Schillers engstem Freund Gottfried Körner Loschwitz

Left: Here Schiller wrote his Ode to Joy
Right: Wineyard Dresden-Loschwitz: sommer residence of Schiller's best friend Gottfried Körner Loschwitz

Justine Segedin das Vorbild für seine Gustel von Blasewitz in „Wallensteins Lager". In Jena, wo Schiller an der Universität Vorlesungen hielt, ist sein damaliges Domizil, das Gartenhaus zu besichtigen und in Weimar schließlich, wo Schiller die letzten und fruchtbarsten Jahre seines Schaffens verbrachte, sein Wohnhaus an der Esplanade (heute Schillerstraße), das Deutsche Nationaltheater, in dem seine Stücke uraufgeführt wurden, mit dem berühmten Goethe-Schiller-Denkmal, die Anna Amalia Bibliothek, der Schiller einen Großteil seines „Lesestoffes" entlieh sowie die Fürstengruft, die letzte Ruhestätte Friedrich Schillers.

Oben links: Schillers Gartenhaus, Jena
Oben rechts: Eingang zu Schillers Wohnhaus, Weimar
Rechts: Goethe-Schiller-Denkmal, Weimar

Segedin, on whom he modelled Gustel of Blasewitz in "Wallenstein's Camp". Jena, where Schiller held lectures at the university, is where he lived at the time in the "Summer House", which can be visited.

Finally Weimar, where Schiller spent the last and most fruitful years of his working life - his house on the Esplanade (today renamed Schiller Street), the German National Theatre with the famous Goethe and Schiller Memorial, where his pieces were first performed, the Anna Amalia Library from which Schiller borrowed a majority of his "reading material", and the Grand Duchal Vault, the last resting place of Friedrich Schiller.

Above left: Schiller's garden house, Jena
Above right: Entrance into Schiller's residential house, Weimar
Right: Goethe-Schiller-monument, Weimar

DEM DICHTERPAAR
GOETHE UND SCHILLER
DAS VATERLAND.

„TAFELGETRÄNK SR. MAJESTÄT“
Radeberger
PILSNER
1905
2005
VOR 100 JAHREN, AM 11. DEZEMBER 1905,
ERKLÄRTE KÖNIG FRIEDRICH AUGUST III. VON SACHSEN
RADEBERGER PILSNER PER DEKRET ZUM
„TAFELGETRÄNK SEINER MAJESTÄT“.

AUF DEN SPUREN DER HANSE

ON THE TRAIL OF THE HANSEATIC LEAGUE

Lübeck & Travemünde
Tourist-Service GmbH
Holstentorplatz 1
23552 Lübeck
Tel.: +49 (0) 1805-882233*
info@luebeck-tourismus.de
www.luebeck-tourismus.de

Bremer Touristik-Zentrale
Findorffstraße 105
28215 Bremen
Tel.: +49 (0) 1805-101030*
info@bremen-tourismus.de
www.bremen-tourismus.de

Tourist-Information Wismar
Am Markt 11
23966 Wismar
Tel.: +49 (0) 3841-2513025
Fax: +49 (0) 3841-2513091
touristinfo@wismar.de
www.wismar.de
Stadtführung:
Tel.: +49 (0) 3841-2513026
Zimmervermittlung:
Tel.: +49 (0) 38 41-2513027

Touristenzentrale
Rostock & Warnemünde
Neuer Markt 3
18055 Rostock
Tel.: +49 (0) 381-19433
+49 (0) 381-2222
Fax: +49 (0) 381-3812601
touristinfo@rostock.de
www.rostock.de

Tourist-Information
Am Strom 59
18119 Rostock-Warnemünde
Tel.: +49 (0) 381-548000
+49 (0) 381-5480010
Fax: +49 (0) 381-5480030

Touristenzentrale
der Hansestadt Stralsund
Alter Markt 9
18439 Stralsund
Tel.: +49 (0) 3831-24690
Fax: +49 (0) 3831-246922
info@stralsundtourismus.de
www.stralsund.de

AUF DEN SPUREN DER MÄRCHENERZÄHLER

ON THE TRAIL OF THE FAIRYTALE STORYTELLERS

Hanau
Tourist–Information
Am Markt 14-18
63450 Hanau
Tel.: +49 (0) 6181-295950
Fax: +49 (0) 6181-295959
touristinformation@hanau.de
www.hanau.de

Marburg Tourismus und Marketing
Pilgrimstein 26
35037 Marburg
Tel.: +49 (0) 6421-99120
Fax: +49 (0) 6421-991212
mtm@marburg.de/mtm
www.marburg.de

*) *Servicenummer der DTAG 0,12 €/min. aus dem Deutschen Festnetz*
*) *Service number of the DTAG 0,12 €/min from the German fixed network*

Fritzlar
Tourist-Information
Zwischen den Krämen 5
34560 Fritzlar
Tel.: +49 (0) 5622-988643
Fax: +49 (0) 5622-988626
touristinfo@fritzlar.de
www.fritzlar.de

Kassel
Tourist-Information im Rathaus
Obere Königstraße 15
34117 Kassel
Tel.: +49 (0) 561-7077107
Fax: +49 (0) 561-7077169
tourist@kassel.de
www.kassel.de

Hofgeismar:
Tourist-Information
Märchenland Reinhardswald
Markt 5
34369 Hofgeismar
Tel.: +49 (0) 5671-5070400
Fax: +49 (0) 5671-500839
touristinfo@stadt-hofgeismar.de
www.hessennet.de/hofgeismar/

Hameln Marketing und
Tourismus GmbH
Deisterallee 1 (am Bürgergarten)
31785 Hameln
Tel.: +49 (0) 1805-515150*
Fax: +49 (0) 5151-957840
touristinfo@hameln.de
www.hameln.de

Stadtmarketing
Horn-Bad Meinberg GmbH
Parkstraße 2
32805 Horn-Bad Meinberg
Tel.: +49 (0) 5234-98903
Fax: +49 (0) 5234-9577
stadtmarketing@horn-badmeinberg.de
www.horn-badmeinberg.de

Für weitere Informationen zu den Externsteinen ist folgende homepage sehr zu empfehlen:
www.externstein.de

Nähere Informationen zum Hermannsdenkmal auch unter
www.hermannsdenkmal.de

Detmold
Touristikinformationen im Rathaus
am Markt
Tel.: +49 (0) 5231-977328
Fax: +49 (0) 5231-977299
tourist.info@detmold.de
www.stadtdetmold.de

Bremer Touristik-Zentrale
Findorffstraße 105
28215 Bremen
Tel.: +49 (0) 1805-101030*
Fax: +49 (0) 421-3080030
info@bremen-tourism.de
www.bremen-tourismus.de

Gästeinformation
Bergstraße 13
27726 Worpswede
Tel.: +49 (0) 4792-935820
Fax: +49 (0) 4792-935823
info@worpswede.de
www.worpswede.de

AUF DEN SPUREN GROSSER KUNSTSAMMLUNGEN

ON THE TRAIL OF LARGE ART COLLECTIONS

Museum Wasserburg Anholt
Schloss 1
46419 Isselburg-Anholt
Tel.: +49 (0) 2874-45353
Fax: +49 (0) 2874-45356
museum@fuerst-salm.de
www.wasserburg-anholt.de

Het Nationale Park de Hoge Veluwe
Apeldoornsweg 250
7351 TA Hoenderloo
Tel.: +31 (0) 318-591627
Fax: +31 (0) 318-592248
informatie@hogeveluwe.nl
www.hogeveluwe.nl

Kröller-Müller-Museum
Houtkampweg 6
6731 AW Otterlo
Tel.: +31 (0) 318-591041
Fax: +31 (0) 318-591515
information@kmm.nl
www.kmm.nl

Museum Schloss Moyland
Am Schloss 4
47551 Bedburg-Hau
Tel.: +49 (0) 2824-951060
Fax: +49 (0) 2824-951094
info@moyland.de
www.moyland.de

Xanten
Tourist Information
Kurfürstenstraße 9
46509 Xanten
Tel.: +49 (0) 2801-98300
Fax: +49 (0) 2801-71664
info@xanten.de
www.xanten.de

Tourist Information
Königstraße 86
47051 Duisburg
Tel.: +49 (0) 203-28 54 40
Fax: +49 (0) 203-28 54 444
service@duisburg-marketing.de
www.duisburg-marketing.de

Stiftung Wilhelm Lehmbruck Museum
Friedrich-Wilhelm-Straße 40
47049 Duisburg
Tel.: +49 (0) 203-2832630
+49 (0) 203-2833294
Fax: +49 (0) 203-28 33 892
info@lehmbruckmuseum.de
www.lehmbruckmuseum.de

Touristikzentrale Essen
Am Hauptbahnhof 2
45127 Essen
Tel.: +49 (0) 201-19433
Fax: +49 (0) 201-8872044
touristikzentrale@essen.de
www.essen.de

Deutsches Plakat Museum
Rathenaustraße 2
45127 Essen
Tel.: +49 (0) 201-8845108
Fax: +49 (0) 201-45122
info@plakatmuseum.essen.de

Museum Folkwang
Goethestraße 41
45128 Essen
Tel.: +49 (0) 201-8845314
+49 (0) 201-8845301
Fax: +49 (0) 201-8845001
info@museumsverwaltung.essen.de
www.museum-folkwang.de

Villa Hügel
Hügel 15
45133 Essen
Tel.: +49 (0) 201-616290
Fax: +49 (0) 201-6162911
office@villahuegel.de
www.villahuegel.de

Zeche Zollverein
Besucherzentrum
Zollverein Schacht XII/Halle 2
Gelsenkirchener Str. 181
45309 Essen
Tel.: +49 (0) 201-8303636
Fax: +49 (0) 201-8303620
besucherzentrum@zollverein.de
www.zollverein.de

Red Dot Design Museum
Gelsenkirchener Str. 181
45309 Essen
Tel.: +49 (0) 201-301040
Fax: +49 (0) 201-3010440
www.red-dot.de

Design Zentrum Nordrhein Westfalen e.V.
Gelsenkirchener Straße 181
45309 Essen
Tel.: +49 (0) 201-301040
Fax: +49 (0) 201-3010440
www.red-dot.de

AUF DEN SPUREN DER ROMANTIK AN MOSEL UND RHEIN

ON THE TRAIL OF ROMANCE ON THE RIVERS MOSEL AND RHEIN

Linksrheinische Strecke:
Boppard
Tourist Information Marktplatz
(Altes Rathaus)
56154 Boppard
Tel.: +49 (0) 6742-3888
Fax: +49 (0) 6742-81402
tourist@boppard.de
www.boppard.de

Trier
Tourist-Information
An der Porta Nigra
54290 Trier
Tel.: +49 (0) 651-978080
Fax: +49 (0) 651-9780888
info@tit.de
www.trier.de

Koblenz
Tourist-Information
Bahnhofplatz 17
56068 Koblenz
Tel.: +49 (0) 261-303880
Fax: +49 (0) 261-3038811
verwaltung@touristik-koblenz.de
www.koblenz.de

Tourist-Information Rathaus
Jesuitenplatz 2
56068 Koblenz
Auskunft und Zimmernachweis
Tel: +49 (0) 261-130920
Kartenvorverkauf
Tel: +49 (0) 261-1291610
Fax: +49 (0) 261-1309211
info-jesuitenpl@touristik-koblenz.de

St. Goar
Heerstraße 86
56329 St. Goar
Tel. +49 (0) 6741-383
Fax +49 (0) 6741-7209
touristinfo@st-goar.de
www.st-goar.de

Oberwesel
Tourist-Information
Rathausstraße 3
55430 Oberwesel
Tel.: +49 (0) 6744-710624
Fax: +49 (0) 6744-1540
info@oberwesel.de
www.oberwesel.de

Barach
Rhein-Nahe Touristik e.V. Bacharach
Oberstraße 45
55422 Bacharach
Tel.: +49 (0) 6743-919303
Fax: +49 (0) 6743-919304
info@rhein-nahe-touristik.de
www.bacharach.de
www.rhein-nahe-touristik.de

Bingen
Tourist-Information
Rheinkai 21
55411 Bingen am Rhein
Te.l: +49 (0) 6721-184205
+49 (0) 6721-184206
+49 (0) 6721-184201
Fax: +49 (0) 6721-184214
tourist-information@bingen.de
www.bingen.de

Bad Kreuznach
Tourist-Information im Haus des Gastes
55543 Bad Kreuznach
Tel. +49 (0) 671- 8360050
Fax: +49 (0) 671-8360085
info@bad-kreuznach-tourist.de
www.stadt-bad-kreuznach.de

Rechtsrheinische Strecke:
Lahnstein:
Tourist-Information
Tel.: +49 (0) 2621-914171
+49 (0) 2621-914172
Fax. +49 (0) 2621-914340
touristinformation@lahnstein.de
www.lahnstein.de

Städtisches Verkehrsamt Kaub
Schulstraße 12
56359 Kaub
Tel.: +49 (0) 6774-222
Fax: +49 (0) 6774-8230
stadt.kaub@t-online.de
www.stadt-kaub.de

Stadtverwaltung Lorch
Hauptstraße 19
73547 Lorch
Tel.: +49 (0) 7172-180119
Fax: +49 (0) 7172-180159
tourist@stadt-lorch.de
www.stadt-lorch.de

Assmannshausen
Tourist-Information siehe Rüdesheim

Rüdesheim
Tourist-Information
Geisenheimer Str. 22
65385 Rüdesheim am Rhein
Tel.: +49 (0) 6722-19433
Fax: +49 (0) 6722-3485
touristinfo@t-online.de
www.ruedesheim.de

Wiesbaden
Tourist Information
Marktstraße 6
65183 Wiesbaden
Tel.: +49 (0) 611-17290
Fax: +49 (0) 611-1729798
tourist-service@wiesbaden.de
www.wiesbaden.de

Zusätzliche Informationen unter:
www.welterbe-mittelrheintal.de

Rhein-Touristik Tal der Loreley
Bahnhofstraße 8
56346 St. Goarshausen
Tel.: +49 (0) 6771-91020
Fax: +49 (0) 6771-91019
info@talderloreley.de
www.tal-der-loreley.de

Weiterführende Informationen zur Nibelungen- und Siegfriedstraße unter:
www.nibelungen-siegfriedstrasse.de

AUF DEN SPUREN DER NIBELUNGEN

ON THE TRAIL OF THE NIBELUNGEN

Touristik-Information Worms
Neumarkt 14
67547 Worms
Tel.: +49 (0) 6241-25045
Fax: +49 (0) 6241-26328
touristinfo@worms.de
www.worms.de

Kultur- und Verkehrsabteilung der Stadt Lorsch
Marktplatz 1
64653 Lorsch
Tel.: +49 (0) 6251-5967400
Fax: +49 (0) 6251-5967400
magistrat-lorsch@t-online.de
www.lorsch.de

Bensheim Touristik-Information
Hauptstraße 39
64625 Bensheim
Tel.: +49 (0) 6251-5826314
Fax: +49 (0) 6251-5826331
touristinfo@bensheim.de
www.bensheim.de

Kur- und Touristikservice Lindenfels
Tel.: +49 (0) 6255-30644
Fax: +49 (0) 6255-30645
touristik@lindenfels.de

Verkehrsamt Michelstadt
Marktplatz 1
64720 Michelstadt
Tel.: +49 (0) 6061-74146
Fax: +49 (0) 6061-706147
stadtverwaltung@michelstadt.de
www.michelstadt.de

Miltenberg Tourist Information Rathaus
Engelplatz
63897 Miltenberg
Tel.: +49 (0) 9371-404119
Fax: +49 (0) 9371-404105
tourismus@miltenberg.de
www.miltenberg.de

Freudenberg Fremdenverkehrsamt
Hauptstraße 152
97896 Freudenberg am Main
Tel.: +49 (0) 9375-920014
Fax: +49 (0) 9375-920050
master@freudenberg-main.de
www.freudenberg-main.de

Würzburg Tourist Information
Falkenhaus am Markt
Tel.: +49 (0) 931-372398
Fax: +49 (0) 931-373952
tourismus@wuerzburg.de
www.wuerzburg.de

Tourist-Information Wertheim
Am Spitzen Turm
97877 Wertheim
Tel.: +49 (0) 9342-1066
Fax: +49 (0) 9342-38277
info@tourist-wertheim.de
www.wertheim.de

Tourist-Information
Stadtverwaltung Tauberbischofsheim
Markplatz 8
97941 Tauberbischofsheim
Tel.: +49 (0) 9341-80313
+49 (0) 9341-80333
Fax: +49 (0) 9341-803991
tourismus@tauberbischofsheim.de
www.tauberbischofsheim.de

Tourist Information
Stadt Walldürn
Verwaltungsgebäude I, Rathaus
Hauptstr. 27
74731 Walldürn
Tel.: +49 (0) 6282-67106
Fax: +49 (0) 6282-67103
waltraud.speth@wallduern.de
www.wallduern.com

Amorbach
Tourist-Information
Altes Rathaus
Marktplatz 1
63916 Amorbach
Tel.: +49 (0) 9373-20940
Fax: +49 (0) 9373-20933
touristinfo@amorbach.de
www.amorbach.de

AUF DEN SPUREN DES JUGENDSTILS

ON THE TRAIL OF ART NOUVEAU

Informationen und Führungen unter:
ProRegio Darmstadt
Stadt- und Touristikmarketing Gesellschaft e. V.
Im Carree 4 A
64283 Darmstadt
Tel.: +49 (0) 6151-9515011
Fax: +49 (0) 6151-9515051
touristikservice@proregio-darmstadt.de
www.darmstadt.de

Literaturtipp
Darmstadt und der Jugendstil
Sachbuchverlag Karin Mader
ISBN 3-921957-22-2

Museum Künstlerkolonie
Alexandraweg 26
64287 Darmstadt
Tel.: +49 (0) 6151-133385
mkkd@darmstadt.de

Ausstellungsgebäude Mathildenhöhe
Sabaisplatz 1
64287 Darmstadt
Tel.: +49 (0) 6151-133350

AUF DEN SPUREN DER PILGER UND MÖNCHE

ON THE TRAIL OF THE PILGRIMS AND THE MONKS

Tourist-Information Speyer
Maximilianstraße 13
67346 Speyer
Tel.: +49 (0) 6232-142392
Fax: +49 (0) 6232-142332
touristinformation@stadt-speyer.de
www.speyer.de

Tourist-Information Priminiusland
„Historama Kloster Hornbach"
Im Klosterbezirk
66500 Hornbach
Tel.: +49 (0) 6338-809153
Fax: +49 (0) 6338-809155
historama-kloster.hornbach1@gmx.de

Für die nördliche Route:
Touristikbüro Kaiserslauterer Land e. V.
Lauterstraße 8
67657 Kaiserslautern
Tel.: +49 (0) 631-7105328
Fax: +49 (0) 631-7105474
klland@kaiserslautern-kreis.de
www.kaiserslautern-kreis.de

Für die südliche Route:
Tourist-Information Südwestpfalz
Unterer Sommerwaldweg 40-42
66953 Pirmasens
Tel.: +49 (0) 6331-809126
Fax: +49 (0) 6331-809202
info@suedwestpfalz-touristik.de
www.suedwestpfalz-touristik.de

Literaturtipp
Pfälzer Jakobswege
Auf historischen
Wegen von Speyer
zum Kloster
Hornbach
Kuntz Verlags GmbH
3. Auflage 2004
ISBN 3-933507-03-0

AUF DEN SPUREN DER STAUFER

ON THE TRAIL OF THE HOUSE OF STAUFER

Tourist-Information Bad Wimpfen-Gundelsheim
Carl-Ulrich Str. 1
74206 Bad Wimpfen
Tel.: +49 (0) 7063-97200
Fax: +49 (0) 7063-972020
info@badwimpfen.org
www.badwimpfen.org

AUF DEN SPUREN FRIEDRICH SCHILLERS

ON THE TRAIL OF FRIEDRICH SCHILLER

Marbach
Tourist-Information
Marktstraße 23
71672 Marbach am Neckar
Tel.: +49 (0) 7144-1020
Fax: +49 (0) 7144-102311
touristik@schillerstadt-marbach.de
www.schillerstadt-marbach.de

Schillers Geburtshaus
Niklastorstraße 31
Tel. +49 (0) 7144-17567
Fax +49 (0) 7144-899671
schillers-geburtshaus@schillerstadt-marbach.de

Deutsches Literaturarchiv
Schillerhöhe 8 – 10
Tel.: +49 (0) 7144-8480
Fax: +49 (0) 7144-848690
museum@dla-marbach.de
www.dla-marbach.de

Ludwigsburg
Tourist Information
Marktplatz 6
71634 Ludwigsburg
Tel.: +49 (0) 7141-9102252
Fax: +49 (0) 7141-9102774
info@stadt.ludwigsburg.de
www.ludwigsburg.de

Schloss Ludwigsburg
Schlossstraße 30
71634 Ludwigsburg
Tel.: +49 (0) 7141-182004
Fax: +49 (0) 7141-186434
info@schloss-ludwigsburg.de
www.schloss-ludwigsburg.de

Bauerbach
Schillermuseum
Hauptstraße 3
Tel.: +49 (0) 36945-50301
Fax: +49 (0) 36945-50692

Begegnungsstätte Friedrich Schiller mit Gaststätte „Zum braunen Ross“
Hinterdorf 73
Telefon: +49 (0) 36945-57374

Naturtheater „Friedrich Schiller“
Tel. & Fax: +49 (0) 36945-50000
www.bauerbach-naturtheater.de

Meiningen
Touristen Information
Markt 14
98617 Meiningen
Tel.: +49 (0) 3693-44650
Fax: +49 (0) 3693-446544
tourist.info@meiningen.de
service@meiningermuseen.de
www.meiningermuseen.de

Literaturmuseum Baumbachhaus
Burggasse 22
98617 Meiningen
Tel.: +49 (0) 3693-502848

Theatermuseum
„Zauberwelt der Kulisse“
Ehemalige Reithalle, Schlossplatz 1
98617 Meiningen
Tel.: +49 (0) 3693-471290
Fax: +49 (0) 3693-9300035

Schloss Elisabethenburg
Schlossplatz 1
98617 Meiningen
Tel.: +49 (0) 3693-881010
Fax: +49 (0) 3693-503644

Meininger Theater
Bernhardstr. 5
98617 Meiningen
Tel.: +49 (0) 3693-451222
+49 (0) 3693-451137
Fax: +49 (0) 3693-451301
kasse@das-meininger-theater.de
www.das-meininger-theater.de

Rudolstadt
Fremdenverkehrsamt
mit Touristinformation
Marktstraße 57
07407 Rudolstadt
Tel.: +49 (0) 3672-424543
+49 (0) 3672-414743
+49 (0) 3672-19433
Fax: +49 (0) 3672-431286
info@rudolstadt.de
www.rudolstadt.de

Schloss Heidecksburg
(Thüringer Landesmuseum)
Schlossbezirk 1
07407 Rudolstadt
Tel.: +49 (0) 3672-42900
Fax: +49 (0) 3672-429090
museum@heidecksburg.de
www.heidecksburg.de

Ehemalige Glockengießerei
Jenaische Str. 1

Leipzig Tourist-Information
Richard-Wagner-Straße 1
04109 Leipzig
Tel.: +49 (0) 341-7104265
Fax: +49 (0) 341-7104271
+49 (0) 341-7104276
Info@LTS-Leipzig.de
www.leipzig.de

Schillerhaus
Menckestraße 42
04155 Leipzig
Tel.: +49 (0) 341-5662170
+49 (0) 341-5662170
stadtmuseum@leipzig.de
www.stadtgeschichtliches-museum-leipzig.de

Dresden
Tourist-Information
Prager Straße, Schinkelwache/Theaterplatz
Ostra-Allee 11, 01067 Dresden
Tel.: +49 (0) 351-49192100
Fax: +49 (0) 351-49192116
info@dresden-tourist.de
www.dresden.de

Schillergarten in Blasewitz/Neugruna
(beim Blauen Wunder)

Jena
Tourist-Information
Johannisstraße 23
07743 Jena
Tel.: +49 (0) 3641-806400
+49 (0) 3641-19433
Fax: +49 (0) 3641-806409
tourist-info@jena.de
www.jena.de

Schillers Gartenhaus
Schillergässchen 2
07745 Jena
Tel.: +49 (0) 3641-931188
Fax: +49 (0) 3641-931187

Weimar
Tourist-Information
Markt 10, 99423 Weimar
Tel.: +49 (0) 3643-7450
Fax: +49 (0) 3643-745420
tourist-info@weimar.de
www.weimar.de

Schillers Wohnhaus
Schillerstraße 12
Tel.: +49 (0) 3643-545350
info@swkk.de
www.swkk.de

Deutsches Nationaltheater
Theaterplatz 2
Tel.: +49 (0) 3643-755334
Fax: +49 (0) 3643-755321
service@nationaltheater-weimar.de
www.nationaltheater-weimar.de

Anna Amalia Bibliothek
Platz der Demokratie 4
Tel.: +49 (0) 3643-545205
Fax: +49 (0) 3643-545829
www.anna-amalia-bibliothek.de

Fürstengruft
Historischer Friedhof Poseckscher Garten
Tel.: +49 (0) 3643-545380
info@swkk.de

REGISTER

BILDNACHWEIS

FotoFabry 6
Gerd Spans 7, 12, 13, 14, 70, 71, 72, 73, 126, 127, 128, 129
Hans van Ooyen 8, 15 (außer oben links), 36 rechts, 37, 60, 61, 62, 63, 64, 65
Schloss Lütgenhof 11, 16, 17, 18, 19
Björn Kray Iversen (Schafhof Amorbach) 15 oben links, 110, 111, 112
Bremer Touristik-Zentrale Gesellschaft für Marketing & Service mbH 20, 38, 44, 45
FOTODESIGN Herzig 21, 22, 23, 24, 28, 29, 93, 101, 102, 103, 104, 105,114, 115, 116 rechts, 117, 159
Touristik Zentrale Stralsund 25, 27
Thomas Radbruch (Lübeck Touristik Information) 26 oben
Hans-Wedig Müller (Lübeck Touristik Information) 26 unten
Burghotel Blomberg 30, 31, 32, 33
Dornröschenschloss Sababurg 34, 35, 36 links
Rainer Kieselbach, Marburg 40
Stadt Kassel 41, 42 rechts
Stadt Hameln 42
Peter Weinfurth www.externstein.de 43
Schloss Waldeck 46, 47, 48, 49
Schloss Spangenberg 50, 51, 52, 53
Parkhotel Wasserburg Anholt 54, 55, 56
Museum Wasserburg Anholt 57, 58
Foto Arnold Meine Jansen 59
Schlosshotel Kurfürstliches Amtshaus 66, 67, 68, 69
Schlosshotel Rheinfels 74, 75, 76, 77
Touristik Information Trier (TI)/Jacobs 78, 79, 80, 81
Koblenz Touristik 82, 83, 84, 88
Willi Knopf, Dielheim 85, 86, 87
Hotel Alte Thorschenke 90, 91, 92
Burghotel Schnellenberg 94, 95, 96, 97
Tourist Information Worms/P. Uhrig 98, 100
Schlosshotel Rothenbuch 106, 107, 108
Kongress und Touristik Betriebe, Aschaffenburg 109
Schafhof Amorbach 113
ProRegio Darmstadt e. V. 116 links
Hotel Jagdschloss Kranichstein 118, 119, 120, 121
Parkhotel Herrenhaus 122, 123, 124, 125
K. Hoffmann 130
Kuntz Verlags GmbH 132, 133
Hotel-Restaurant Burg Hornberg 134, 135, 136, 137
Tourist Information Bad Wimpfen 138, 139
Hotel Eisenhut 140, 141, 142, 143
Schloss Steinburg 144, 145, 146, 147
Schloss Landsberg 148, 149, 150, 151
Falko Behr 152, 153, 154, 155, 156, 157, 158, 160
Wassersportcenter Sun&Fun Edertal-Edersee 49

Bild-, Quellennachweis

Das Copyright für die abgebildeten Werke liegt, sofern nachfolgend nichts anderes aufgeführt ist, bei den jeweiligen Fotografen, Touristik-Informationen und Hotels. Die Fotos der einzelnen Hotels wurden uns von diesen zur Verfügung gestellt.
Trotz intensiver Recherche ist nicht auszuschließen, dass in jedem Fall die Urheberrechte ermittelt wurden. Wir bitten ggf. um Mitteilung an den Verlag.

Alle in diesem Buch enthaltenen Angaben wurden von den Autoren nach bestem Wissen erstellt und von ihnen und dem Verlag mit größtmöglicher Sorgfalt überprüft. Gleichwohl sind inhaltliche Fehler nicht vollständig auszuschließen. Daher erfolgen die Angaben im Sinne der Produkthaftung ohne jegliche Verpflichtung oder Garantie des Verlages oder der Autoren. Beide übernehmen keinerlei Verantwortung und Haftung für etwaige inhaltliche Unstimmigkeiten. Wir bitten dafür um Verständnis und werden Korrekturhinweise gerne aufgreifen. **info@reiseart.com**

Picture Credits and References

The copyright for the reproduced work is, if nothing different is subsequently specified, owned by the respective photographers, tourist information offices and hotels. The photographs of the individual hotels were made available to us by these sources.
Despite having done intensive research, it is not to be ruled out that in each case the copyrights were in fact acquired. We ask if this is found to be the case that it be reported to the publishing house.

All the data quoted in this book was supplied by the authors to the best of their knowledge and the greatest possible care was taken by them and the publishing house to verify the accuracy of the data. Nevertheless the possible occurrence of errors in the content is not to be completely dismissed. Therefore the data in the sense of product liability is provided without any obligation or guarantee from the publishing house or the authors. Neither take any responsibility and liability for any discrepancies in the content. We therefore ask for understanding and will gladly look into queries regarding possible corrections to be made. **info@reiseart.com**